Windows XP Embedded Step by Step

Windows XP Embedded Step by Step

by James Beau Cseri

RTC Books

San Clemente

Windows XP Embedded Step-by-Step
By James Beau Cseri

Published by

RTC Books
927 Calle Negocio Suite G
San Clemente, CA 92673

http://www.rtcbooks.com

Printed in the United States of America
ISBN 0-929392-73-6
First Printing January 2003

We welcome your comments. Email us at books@rtcgroup.com Errata and clarifications will be posted to www.rtcbooks.com.

Dedication

To my best friend, my love, and my soul mate, Jayna Lynn

Contents

CHAPTER 1 Introduction to Windows XP Embedded 1

Introduction *1*

Overview *2*

Reliability, Security, Speed *3*

Full-featured *4*

Connected *5*

Rapid Development *6*

About this book *7*

System Requirements – Please Read! *7*

Development System *8*

Target System *9*

Additional requirements *10*

CHAPTER 2 The Build Overview 11

Building and Deploying the Run-time Image *12*

The Build Process *12*

Deployment *15*

The Target Media *15*

Media Structure *16*

Preparing the Target Media *16*

Transferring the Run-time Image *17*

The First Boot Agent 18
System Cloning 19
Build Options 20
Licensing a Run-time Image 20

CHAPTER 3 Development Kit Installation 23

Tools Setup 23
Database Engine Setup 25
Database Setup 26
Installation Scenarios 26
EXERCISE 1A 29
EXERCISE 1B 40

CHAPTER 4 Component Database Manager 45

The Database Tab 46
EXERCISE 2 48
The Platform Tab 50
The Package Tab 51
The Component Tab 52
Filter Tool 53
EXERCISE 3 54
Windows XP Embedded Updates 58
EXERCISE 4 58

CHAPTER 5 Target Analyzer 65

Overview 65

EXERCISE 5 69

CHAPTER 6 Target Designer 75

Target Designer Overview 75

Component Browser 76

Configuration Editor 79

Details Pane 81

Output Pane 83

Target Designer Options 84

Mode 85

Build 86

Dependency Check 87

Advanced 88

EXERCISE 6 89

EXERCISE 7 90

Troubleshooting Tips 100

The Windows XP Embedded Desktop 102

CHAPTER 7 Component Designer 105

Typical Object Properties 107

Repositories 110

Creation and Use of Repositories in the Build Process 111
Repository Properties and Resources 112
Repository Sets 112
Packages 113
Components 113
Component Properties 114
Group Memberships 117
Files 118
Registry Data 121
Component or Group Dependency 124
Build Order Dependency 125
Resources 126
Dependencies 129
EXERCISE 8 131
EXERCISE 9 140

CHAPTER 8 Embedded Enabling Features 145

Shell Customization 145
Headless Operation 147
Headless Design Considerations 147
Remote Management 148
EXERCISE 10 150
System Message Interception 155

EXERCISE 11 .... *156*
Enhanced Write Filter *165*
- *Overlay Types* *166*
- *EWF Volume* *167*
- *EWF Components and Files* *167*
- *Enhanced Write Filter Settings* *168*

EXERCISE 12 .... *171*
Flash Media *180*
El Torito Bootable CD-ROM *180*
EXERCISE 13 .... *182*

CHAPTER 9 Advanced Component Authoring Techniques **195**

Component Conversion *195*
Importing a PMQ file *196*
- *Importing an INF file* *196*
- *Importing a KDF file* *197*

Component Authoring Tools and Techniques *198*
- *System Snapshot Tools* *198*
- *File System Monitoring: Filemon* *200*
- *Registry Monitoring: Regmon* *201*
- *File Dependencies* *202*

EXERCISE 14 .... *203*
EXERCISE 15 .... *209*

CHAPTER 10 Appendix A 217

CHAPTER 1 Introduction to Windows XP Embedded

Section 1.1 Introduction

Microsoft's Windows XP Embedded provides an outstanding foundation for building embedded systems. The componentized version of Windows XP and the successor of Windows NT Embedded 4.0, Windows XP Embedded enables the rapid development of reliable and full-featured connected embedded devices. Windows XP Embedded is built from the same code base as Windows XP, so many features are inherited from Windows XP. For example, application development is virtually identical for both operating systems, thanks to the same underlying binaries. And because of its full Win32 API support, existing off-the-shelf applications and drivers can be used with little or no porting required. Rapid application development can be achieved using familiar tools, such as Visual Studio, to write full-featured applications.

The use of embedded computing devices has seen a tremendous increase in recent years. They've found their way into a number of applications, including retail point of sale devices, kiosks and ATMs, office automation equipment, such as printers and copiers, industrial automation, medical systems test equipment, network devices including routers and switches, database and multimedia servers and communication systems, among many others.

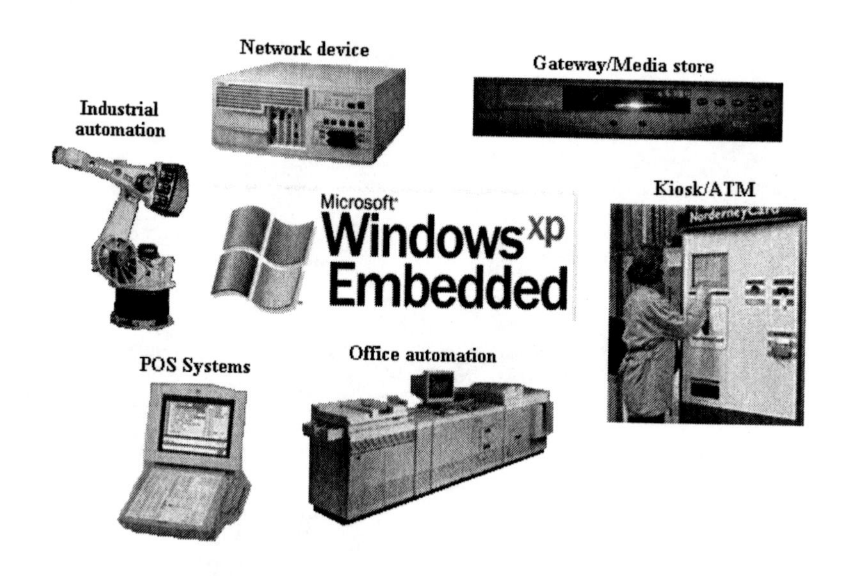

Figure 1.1 Example device scenarios.

These devices create new opportunities for enterprises to empower employees, connect to customers, and integrate with partners and suppliers. In order for end-to-end business solutions to be fully brought to fruition, smart devices are required to meet the needs of developers as well as end users.

Section 1.2 Overview

Windows XP Embedded features several improvements over NT Embedded in order to live up to its key claims of being reliable, full-featured, connected, and rapidly developed.

Section 1.2.1 Reliability, Security, Speed

Today's mission critical embedded systems must be as reliable as possible, and this is one of the key strengths of Windows XP Embedded. Windows XP Embedded includes features designed to support a system requiring high uptime:

- Windows File Protection - Prevents core system files from being overwritten by application installations; the correct version of the file will be restored.

- Device Driver Rollback - Saves the previous version of a driver when a new driver is installed. If there are any issues with the newer driver, the original driver can be re-installed.

- Windows Driver Protection - Prevents accidental installation and loading of defective drivers. An error message is instead presented along with a link to web page containing more information.

- Windows Update - Delivers critical operating system updates which can optionally be automatically downloaded and installed.

The increasing sophistication of hackers and the business costs associated with malicious intruders necessitates an OS which emphasizes security. Windows XP Embedded enables developers to implement local and network security with support for industry standards, such as Kerberos authentication protocol, Internet Protocol Security (IPSec), and Internet firewall. Support is also provided for many security related settings, such as user access permissions, which can be implemented individually to protect selected files, applications, and other resources. To manage security policy on your computer, organizational unit, or domain, XP Embedded includes a set of tools through the security configuration manager. Improved security also means that there are more implementation possibilities that ever before.

The performance of Windows XP Embedded has been improved significantly. The pre-emptive multi-tasking architecture of XP Embedded was designed to allow multiple applications to run simultaneously, with enhancements to ensure great system response and stability. Enhanced memory management ensures the right pages are being pre-fetched from the disk based on the application usage. Improvements to the boot loader accelerate driver response time and registry initialization. XP Embedded accelerates the boot process by pre-fetching much of the OS at the same time that devices are being initialized, rather than running consecutively.

Section 1.2.2 Full-featured

Windows XP Embedded provides over 10,000 components, which are individual OS features, services, and drivers, to develop your customized, reduced footprint embedded device. A Windows XP Embedded image footprint can be as small as 5 or 6 megabytes (a very minimal, kernel baseline configuration which includes the kernel, but not network support or an explorer shell). The size of the footprint depends on the functionality added to the image.

By including the appropriate components in a build, the full Win32 API support enables any application that can run on Windows XP to run on Windows XP Embedded. XP Embedded uses the same Windows Driver Model as Windows XP. This enables all existing Windows XP drivers to be easily used on a Windows XP Embedded build. New device support includes support for a wide array of Universal Serial Bus peripherals such as scanners, mice, keyboards, and more, and Plug and Play for automatic discovery, configuration, and installation of devices without user intervention.

The latest multimedia and web browsing capabilities are also featured in XP Embedded. This includes Internet Explorer 6, Windows Media Player 8, DirectX 8, and Broadcast Driver Architecture, which defines a framework that supports various component topologies for receiving digital and analog television.

In addition to the ability to selectively build functionality into the system, XP Embedded includes embedded specific features to meet the unique requirements of embedded designs. These embedded enabling features include, among many others:

- Booting and running from alternative non-volatile media, such as CD-ROM, DiskOnChip, and Flash.

- Enhanced Write Filter technology, which allows the operating system to boot and run from read-only media.

- Headless operation, for systems that do not require a display, keyboard, or mouse.

- Remote management, which not only enables a user to remotely administer a device, but also provides a facility that can be used to acknowledge system error messages without user interaction.

- A custom shell can be used instead of the default Windows Explorer shell, for devices that are strictly dedicated to an application.

Section 1.2.3 Connected

Embedded systems today increasingly require sophisticated connectivity, and XPE provides a full slate of features. The incorporated capabilities of XP Embedded provide easy integration with PCs, servers, and other devices. Support is also included for the leading networking technologies, including legacy network support, IrDA, 802.11 high bandwidth wireless LAN technology, Universal Plug and Play, Remote Desktop Protocol, and Internet connection sharing, which enables multiple devices to share a single internet connection.

The real-time communications support of XP Embedded includes TAPI 3.1, Microsoft Message Queuing support, Outlook Express (which includes greater protection from email viruses), Windows messenger that can use text, voice, or video to communicate real-time with others, and NetMeeting for internet conferencing and application sharing. In addition, XP Embedded supports local and remote management with built in support for Windows Management Instrumentation and Microsoft Management Console, along with Terminal Services.

Section 1.2.4 Rapid Development

To enable faster time-to-market, Windows XP Embedded provides a set of development tools and utilities that make operating system customization and building relatively easy. Development for common devices can often be jump started using one of the provided design templates as a starting point.

The Windows Embedded Studio tool set includes:

- Target Analyzer – Probes the target device hardware and analyzes its contents, ensuring that your run-time image will support your chosen hardware.

- Target Designer – Provides a development environment used to create a bootable run-time image for the device. Target Designer features an automated build process, advanced component browsing and automated dependency checking to ensure that the appropriate components are included to build the run-time image.

- Component Designer – Provides a graphical development environment used to create a component which may include a driver, application, service, or other custom feature that can be included in the operating system build. Component Designer has the ability to convert any device INF file into a component.

- Component Database Manager – Provides a graphical interface and functions used to manage the component database and files.

- Bootprep – Used to prepare target media (hard disk, flash, etc.) for booting Windows XP Embedded.

Note: Windows NT Embedded 4.0 developers will notice that the two primary XP Embedded authoring tools, Target Designer and Component Designer, use the same name as their NT Embedded predecessors. The XP Embedded tools are not the same as the NT Embedded tools and cannot be substituted.

Due to full Win32 API support, existing off-the-shelf applications and drivers can be used with little or no porting required. Rapid application development can be achieved using familiar tools, such as Visual Studio (which is used by over 6 million developers world wide), to write full-featured applications.

Section 1.3 About this book

Although there are many topics within the scope of Windows XP, the area of interest for this book is Windows XP Embedded. The focus is on the use of the tools used to create a Windows XP Embedded operating system, as well as topics specific to embedded systems. The chapters and exercises are designed for users that have little or no experience in developing Windows XP Embedded operating systems. You might find that the exercises may not cover your specific development requirement, but they will cover the general development process and concepts to get you on your way. Each chapter and exercise builds on the former in order to demonstrate a concept or feature of Windows XP Embedded.

Note: Because later exercises often build upon preceding exercises you are strongly encouraged to complete each exercise in order, even if some of the initial exercises appear simple. The initial files created will be used several times throughout the book.

Through hands-on learning, the exercises will step you through installing the development tools, building a run-time images, creating components, making use of the embedded enabling features, and using alternative techniques to help author a component. Some of the exercises demonstrate more than one concept or topic.

Section 1.4 System Requirements – Please Read!

In order to build and run a Windows XP Embedded operating system, you will need the Windows XP Embedded development kit. An evaluation version of the kit is available for a nominal fee ($9.00-$13.00). Information on obtaining the

Windows XP Embedded development kit can be found at http://www.microsoft.com/embedded.

In addition, the development system and target system must meet certain requirements.

Section 1.4.1 Development System

The minimum requirements of the development system vary according to the installation scenario. There are two possible installation scenarios: a client/server installation and a stand-alone installation. The details of each will be covered in Chapter 3. In a client/server installation, the client machine can be running Windows 2000 with Service Pack 2 (SP2) or later, or Windows XP Professional, and must have the minimum hardware requirements of a 500 MHz CPU, 128 MB of RAM, 200 MB of disk space, and a 300 MB page file. The server in the client/server installation must be running Windows 2000 Server and Microsoft SQL Server 2000, and meet the minimum hardware requirements of a 500 MHz CPU, 256 MB of RAM, 3 GB of disk space, and a 600 MB page file. The stand-alone installation must run Windows 2000 SP2 or later, or Windows XP Professional, and meet the minimum hardware requirements of a 500 MHz CPU, 256 MB of RAM, 3 GB of disk space, and a 600 MB page file.

These are the recommended minimum requirements for the development system. For significantly improved performance, a 1 GHz or better CPU is recommended and at least 512 MB of RAM is recommended. Except for the server in the client/server installation, it is recommended that the development system run Windows XP Professional, simply because certain settings can be copied into a Windows XP Embedded run-time image from the development OS. The exercises assume that the development system is running Windows XP Professional.

Section 1.4.2 Target System

Typically, the XP Embedded operating system would be built and deployed to a target device, such as a single board computer. For the sake of simplicity and to keep your costs down, the exercises in this book assume that the development machine itself will be used as the target device, and therefore a second partition needs to exist. The second partition will be used as the XP Embedded target drive and the system will be set up for a dual-boot scenario in Exercise 6 of the Target Designer chapter. At the outset all that is required is a second FAT partition that is between 500 MB and 2 GB in size. Also, one of the later exercises will require there to be a small amount of unallocated space, so around 100 MB of disk space should remain unallocated.

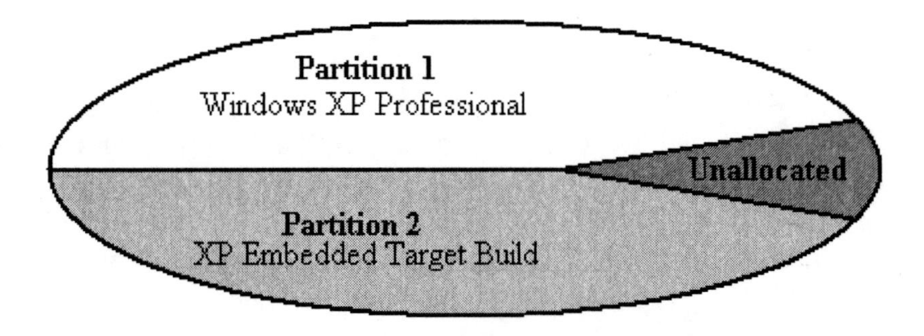

Figure 1.2 Partition setup for this book's exercises.

The exercises can still be completed if a separate target device is used. The target device can even be another desktop PC, but it must meet the following minimum hardware requirements:

- Intel Pentium II or higher (300 MHz or higher) CPU.
- PCI 2.0 or higher recommended.

- Advanced Configuration and Power Interface Plug and Play BIOS recommended.
- Storage depends on the functionality built into the OS. 5 MB meets the minimum requirement for a kernel baseline configuration. For the exercises in this book, a conservative minimum of 650 MB is recommended.
- Amount of RAM depends on the functionality built into the OS. 64 MB is the recommended minimum, but more should be included for increased performance.

Section 1.4.3 Additional requirements

Some exercises have additional hardware and software requirements. In one exercise you will create a Windows XP Embedded image that will boot and run from a CD-ROM. This will require you to have a CD burner, some blank CDs, and CD burning software that enables you to create an ISO-9660 CD from an ISO-9660 image file. *You need to make certain that your software will create ISO-9660 CDs.* For this exercise, you will also need an additional, clean hard disk in addition to the hard disk in the development system. This is because prior to being burned onto a CD, the XP Embedded run-time image must first boot from the *first* partition of the additional drive. See Chapter 8 for more details.

Other exercises use third party software that can be downloaded for free from the internet:

- Scanbin (Jean-Claude Bellamy): http://www.bellamyjc.net/en/scanbin.html
- Filemon (Sysinternals): http://www.sysinternals.com
- Regmon (Sysinternals): http://www.sysinternals.com

CHAPTER 2 The Build Overview

Building a Windows XP Embedded operating system (OS) is a fairly straightforward process using a variety of tools provided by Windows Embedded Studio. The tools in the Windows Embedded Studio toolset can help determine the hardware components of the device, prepare the target media, create custom features for the operating system, and build a customized operating system. Most of the work of building the customized operating system is done by the tools, enabling developers to focus more on designing the system to meet the requirements of the end user, rather than spending time on implementation. After becoming familiar with the build process and learning how to use the tools, experience comes fairly quickly and easily.

The areas of focus for this chapter will include an overview of the build process, deployment to the target media, the boot process, and the build options. Details of the build process steps will be covered throughout the rest of the book.

Section 2.1 Building and Deploying the Run-time Image

A component is a piece of functionality that can be included in an OS configuration. It can include settings, files, registry data, and even other components. The componentized version of Windows XP, Windows XP Embedded keeps all of the components used to make up the operating system in a database. In general, building the operating system involves using the tools provided by Windows Embedded Studio to create, edit, and collect components to piece together a run-time image.

Section 2.1.1 The Build Process

The very first step in creating a custom OS is to determine the individual hardware devices that constitute the target computer. Windows Embedded Studio includes a console utility called Target Analyzer that gathers information about the hardware on the target computer and produces a file, called a PMQ file, containing the results of the find.

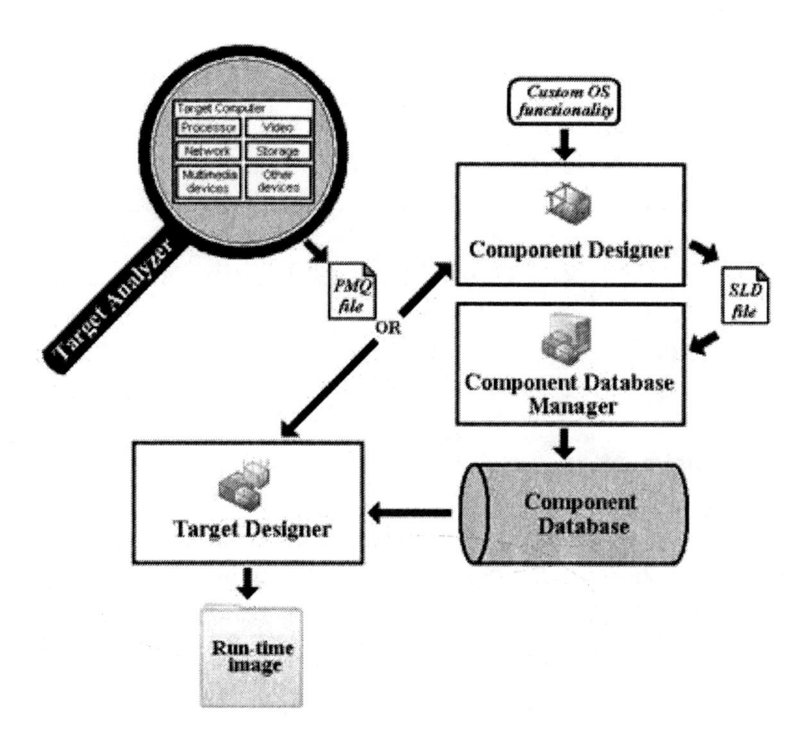

Figure 2.1 The build process.

The results of Target Analyzer can be used to create a base configuration as a starting point. A configuration is a set of data that contains all of the information necessary to build a run-time operating system image. Configurations are created and edited using Target Designer, and can be saved as a System Level Configuration (SLX) file. A new configuration does not contain any data until data is added to it. However, Target Designer can read the Target Analyzer results file and add all the hardware components to the configuration based on what Target Analyzer found.

An alternative method of including all of the components discovered by Target Analyzer is to create a component based on the Target Analyzer results file. Components are created and edited using Component Designer. Component Designer can read the Target Analyzer results file and combine all of the hardware components into one component. This enables the target computer to be treated as one single device by the development tools, even though there may be many individual devices that collectively make up the target computer.

A component needs to be created for any OS feature, such as a device driver or an application, and then imported into the component database before it can be included in an OS configuration. In addition to being able to create a component from a PMQ file, Component Designer can also be used to create a custom component for a particular OS feature that has not already been componentized. The results of Component Designer are imported into the component database using Component Database Manager. Once in the component database, the component can be included in the Target Designer OS configuration.

The hardware components detected by Target Analyzer can be brought into a Target Designer OS configuration directly by importing the PMQ file, or by converting the PMQ file into a component, importing the component into the component database, and then including the component in the Target Designer configuration.

The next step following the creation of a base configuration is to add the desired functionality to the OS by including the appropriate software components in the configuration. The component database includes several design template components, which can add functionality to the OS based on an existing technology, such as a retail point-of-sale terminal, a set top box, or an internet appliance, to name a few.

After all of the desired components have been added to the Target Designer OS configuration, dependency checks must be performed on the configuration. Dependency checks examine the components in the configuration and determine if the components require any other components, which are not already in the configuration, in order to function properly.

Once all of the required components have been included into the configuration through dependency checks, the configuration is ready to be used to build a run-time image. Target Designer examines the components and settings of the configuration and builds the run-time image to a specified build destination folder in the development machine's file system. After the target media has been prepared, the final step in the build process is to transfer the run-time image from the build destination folder on the development system to the target media, then boot the system.

Section 2.1.2 Deployment

Deployment of the operating system involves determining the type of media that the target device is to use and then transferring the operating system to the target media. There are extra steps required in order to deploy a Windows XP Embedded run-time image to a CD-ROM or to a DiskOnChip. If the image is to be deployed to a CD-ROM, certain components must be built into the run-time image and certain settings must be modified, such as disabling the page file. Prior to burning the run-time image onto a CD, it must first run on a hard disk so that the operating system can initialize itself on the very first boot. After that, a couple of utilities are used to prepare the image to be burned on the CD. The details and steps in creating a Windows XP Embedded bootable CD-ROM will be covered and demonstrated in an exercise in the Embedded Enabling Features chapter.

When deploying the run-time image to M-Systems' DiskOnChip, a True Flash File System (TrueFFS) driver must be built into the image. Windows XP Embedded includes the M-Systems' TrueFFS driver component, which is located on the Windows XP Embedded Studio CD in the folder \VALUEADD\3RDPARTY\MSYSTEMS\. When deploying to any other flash device, such as CompactFlash, as long as the BIOS is able to recognize the flash device as an AT disk, there are no special requirements and it can be treated like any hard disk.

Section 2.2 The Target Media

In order to grasp what happens when the target media is prepared for booting a Windows XP Embedded operating system, it is helpful to have an understanding of the structure of the target media.

Section 2.2.1 Media Structure

All disks used to boot any Windows operating system consist of a Master Boot Record (MBR) and partitions. The Master Boot Record is the very first sector on the hard disk. It consists of the Master Partition Table, which contains information about the partition structure of the disk, and a small piece of code called the Master Boot Code, which helps start the process of booting the computer by searching for a partition which is flagged as bootable.

The disk is divided into partitions. A partition is a portion of the disk that functions as though it were physically separate. The Master Partition Table in the MBR allows up to four partitions to exist on a disk: up to four primary partitions or up to three primary partitions and one extended partition. After a primary partition is created, it must be formatted with a file system and have a drive letter assigned to it before data can be stored on it, then it becomes referred to as a volume. An extended partition can be used when you need to have more than four volumes on a disk. Unlike a primary partition, the extended partition is not formatted with a file system and assigned a drive letter. Instead, a logical drive is created within the extended partition, and then the logical drive is formatted with a file system and assigned a drive letter. An unlimited number of logical drives can be created on a basic disk.

Section 2.2.2 Preparing the Target Media

Before the run-time image can be copied to the target media, some steps must be taken to prepare the target media for booting the Windows XP Embedded OS. Preparing the target media can be achieved in two ways. For the first method, the target media can be physically connected to the development system and the Windows disk tools can be used. The target media can be a separate disk, or a second partition can be created on the development system disk using the Windows disk tools, and the system can be set up as a dual boot system. The system will be able to boot up either the development OS (Windows 2000/XP Pro) or the Windows XP Embedded OS. The dual-boot setup will be described in the Target Designer chapter.

The other method of preparing the target media is to use a DOS boot floppy with the DOS disk tools fdisk and format, and boot the target system to DOS so that the tools can be used on the target media. The DOS method uses fdisk.exe as the disk tool and requires the use of bootprep.exe, a utility which is included with Windows Embedded Studio. The procedure will be described below.

The first step is to create a partition on the disk from unallocated space. The disk must be marked as active if it is a separate disk from the development system's disk. If the disk is not an AT disk, such as a DiskOnChip, then third party utilities may need to be used to create partitions or format the media. OEMs typically supply such utilities. After the partition is created, it must be formatted to the FAT file system. The next step is to install the Master Boot Record by booting the system to a DOS boot floppy that contains the fdisk.exe utility. The command for creating an MBR is **fdisk /mbr**. The final step before the run-time image can be copied onto the volume is to create a partition boot sector that will boot Windows XP Embedded. This is done by using the bootprep.exe utility included with Windows Embedded Studio. Usage of the bootprep.exe utility can be displayed by typing **bootprep /?**.

If the target disk can be physically connected to the development system, all of the steps can be achieved using the disk manager in the Windows desktop OS. It can be brought up by right-clicking **My Computer**, selecting **Manage**, and then clicking **Disk Management**. By right-clicking on the unallocated space in the display, the **New partition** wizard will step you though creating a new partition and take care of everything that needs to be done to the disk in order for it to run Windows XP Embedded.

Section 2.2.3 Transferring the Run-time Image

There are two methods that can be used to transfer a run-time image from the build destination folder on the development system to the target media. The first method is to physically connect the disk to the development system. Jumpers on the disk may have to be configured to set the disk up as a slave device depending on exactly how the disk is connected to the system. Sometimes this is the only method available for copying the run-time image to the target media.

The other method involves using third party tools to establish a remote connection to the device and access the media. Winternals provides such a tool, Remote Recover, which is available for purchase at http://www.winternals.com. This tool requires that the target system is equipped with a floppy disk drive and a network adapter. No operating system is needed on the target system in order to map the target hard drive to the development system over the network. A client floppy boot disk that is specific to the target device is created by Remote Recover and then the target device is booted using that floppy disk. Remote Recover runs on the development system and waits for the target device to show up on the network. When the device does appear, the target drive can be mounted so that it will appear in the development system's file explorer like any local disk does, and files can be copied to the mounted drive in the same manner as copying files to another local folder. Remote Recover is able to copy files to the target system, preserving the long file names. If a regular network enabled DOS boot floppy is used to transfer files between the target system and the development system, the long file names are truncated to the 8.3 format, which may cause the OS to not function properly, especially if the file happens to be an important system file that the OS requires.

Section 2.3 The First Boot Agent

On the first boot of the system immediately following the deployment of the run-time image, the First Boot Agent runs, performing any run-time tasks that could not be performed offline with the development tools. The FBA acts as the Windows installer for Windows XP Embedded, performing several of the same tasks such as Plug and Play detection, security installation, network configuration, catalog registration, dynamic link library (DLL) registration, and profile initialization. The operating system is not fully functional until the FBA successfully completes these tasks.

Section 2.4 System Cloning

When a run-time image is to be cloned to several identical target devices, such as in a manufacturing environment, the **System Cloning Tool** component must be included. Every system must have a unique Security ID (SID), which is an identifier that is used to identify user, group, and computer accounts on a network. The System Cloning Tool component ensures that the run-time image on each device has a unique SID.

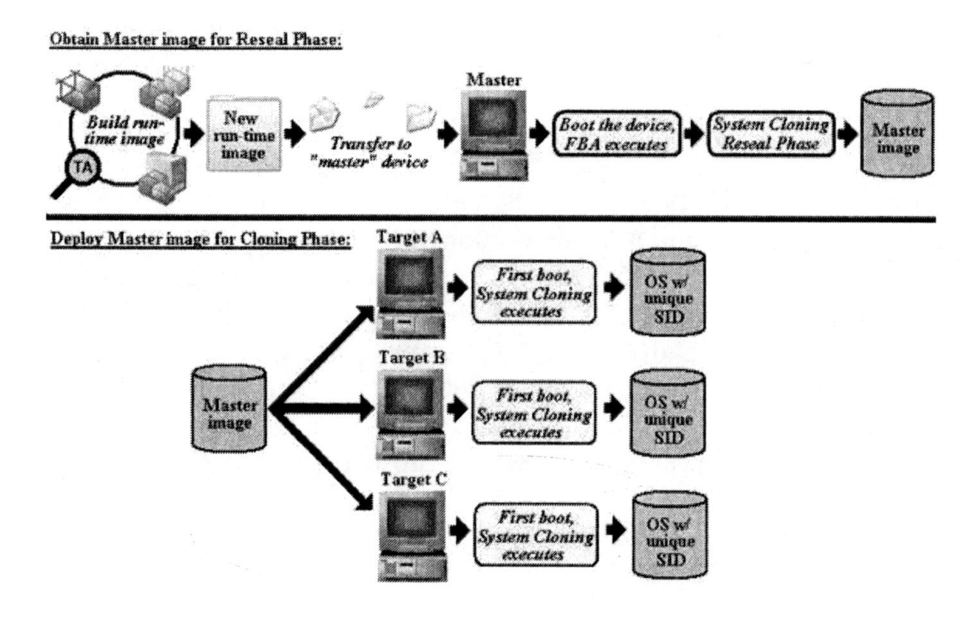

Figure 2.2 An overview of the System Cloning process.

The system cloning process starts by using the Windows Embedded Studio tools to create a configuration and build a run-time image, which must include the System Cloning Tool component. The run-time image is then transferred to one of the clone devices, which will be considered the "master" device. The master device is booted so that the First Boot Agent can execute, performing the system initialization. After the First Boot Agent completes, the run-time image is put into a Reseal phase. When the system is put into Reseal phase, the run-time image is ready to be deployed to the other clone devices. Upon the first boot after the image is put into Reseal phase, the System Cloning tool will assign a unique Security ID.

A message box appears after the FBA completes, indicating that the image is in Reseal and asking if you wish to reboot. At this point, the system can be turned off. However, the system can be rebooted and further configured prior to putting it into Reseal. When the system reboots, a unique SID will be assigned to the system and the system can be configured as desired. When done configuring, the **fbreseal.exe** application located in the folder **\Windows\System32** can be executed to put the system back into the Reseal phase.

Section 2.5 Build Options

Windows XP Embedded operating system has the option of being built as a debug version or a release version. A debug version of the operating system is built using debug versions of files, where applicable, which have extra debugging information built into them. The debug version of the operating system is used to debug applications and device drivers during the development process and should not be deployed outside of the development environment. The release version is built using the final release versions of the files that make up the operating system and is used when the system is ready for manufacturing deployment.

Section 2.5.1 Licensing a Run-time Image

Part of preparing the operating system for its final deployment to manufacturing is to provide the proper licensing information in the run-time image build. Whether it is a release build or a debug build, the operating system will be considered a *test build* without a product identification key included in the run-time image build. A test build will expire between 90 and 180 days. After this time period elapses a blue screen with a STOP message will appear when attempting to boot the OS, and the OS will no longer boot. It is important to synchronize the system clocks on the development machine and the target machine to help keep track of when the expiration will occur.

To ensure that the XP Embedded operating system will not expire, a product id key must be entered in the configuration's settings in Target Designer (instructions on how this can be done will be explained in the Target Designer chapter). The product id key is obtained by purchasing a Windows XP Embedded operating system license from Microsoft or an authorized distributor. A list of authorized distributors can be found on Microsoft's embedded web site, http://www.microsoft.com/embedded. When purchasing several Windows XP Embedded operating system licenses, one product id key could be issued to cover several OS serial numbers. For example, if 100 Windows XP Embedded operating system licenses were purchased for an XP Embedded run-time image which is to be deployed to 100 identical devices, the one product id key could be issued to represent a range of 100 OS serial numbers. This is far more convenient than building the same run-time image 100 times using 100 different product id keys. Windows XP Embedded is activated using the Windows Product Activation (WPA) technology infrastructure. Unlike desktop versions of Windows XP, XP Embedded does not allow on-line activation of the OS, so Internet access is not required to activate the system; end-user interaction is not required. Activation is handled internally when a proper product id key is typed into the configuration settings.

With the feature and build overview complete, you will be guided though hands-on use of the development tools used to create a Windows XP Embedded run-time operating system image. The chapter that follows will step you though the installation of the Windows Embedded Studio tool set and provide an overview of the tools provided.

CHAPTER 3 Development Kit Installation

Section 3.1 Tools Setup

Executing the Tools Setup will install Windows Embedded Studio, which is the set of development tools you use to customize your Windows XP Embedded operating system according to the requirements of your hardware or software.

There are three steps to installing the development kit:

- Tools Setup
- Database Engine Setup
- Database Setup

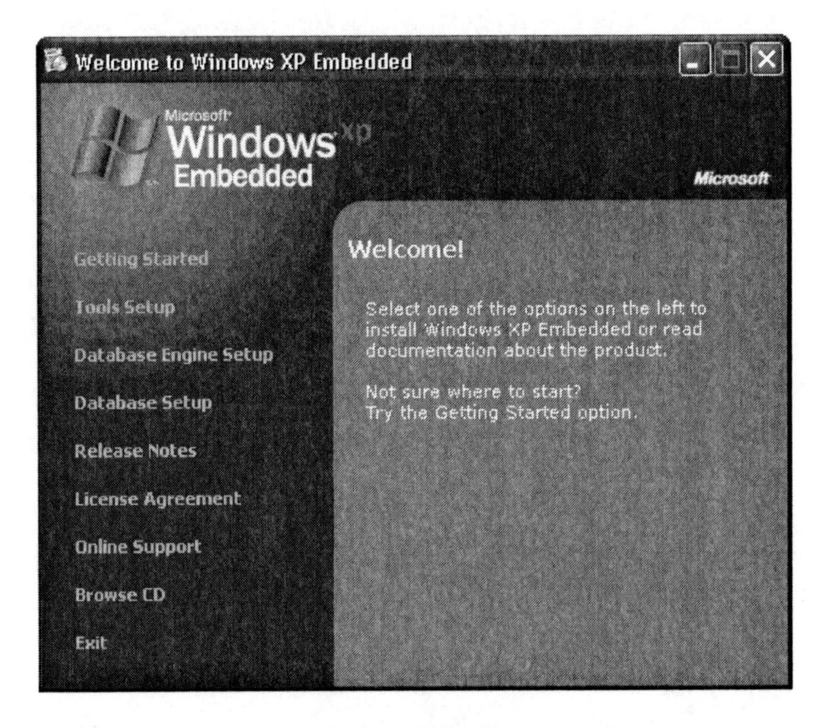

Figure 3.1 The setup screen as it appears when the Windows XP Embedded CD is inserted.

After completing the Tools Setup, the following will be installed on your system (each will be discussed in further detail later in the book):

- Target Designer - This development environment is the main tool for building custom operating systems. You can browse the component database (a filter tool is included), create a configuration for the target device, add the necessary components for the target application, check dependencies to make sure the configuration has the appropriate components to create your run-time image, and build the run-time image.

- Component Designer - Component Designer is a development environment used to author components and prepare your application to be included in a run-time image. A component consists of files, registry entries, and dependencies upon other components.

- Component Database Manager - The Component Database Manager is an interface tool that provides management functions for the database and repositories which are used by the Target Designer and Component Designer tools. Within the Component Database Manager tool, you can import component definition files created by Component Designer, remove database objects, select a component database server to work with both Target Designer and Component Designer, set up repositories, and change the repository search path.

- Documentation and Help - The help system can be launched from the desktop Start menu or it can be launched from Target Designer, Component Designer, or the Component Database Manager.

In addition, some useful development command line utilities are installed:

- Target Analyzer (ta.exe or tap.exe) comes in two versions and can be used to automatically probe your target system to produce a list of Plug and Play identifiers for every device that is detected on the target system. A results file is produced, which can be imported into Target Designer or Component Designer.

- Bootprep.exe is used to prepare your target media for booting Windows XP Embedded after formatting and preparing the active partition to boot on the media using FAT, BIGDOS FAT 16, or FAT 32.

- SDI Manager is a tool that enables you to deploy your run-time image onto a disk or disk partition.

Section 3.2 Database Engine Setup

The Database Engine Setup will install the Microsoft SQL Server Database Engine (MSDE). MSDE is a client/server data engine that provides local data storage on a single-user computer or small workgroup server, and is compatible with Microsoft SQL Server. For a client/server installation, the component database server will need to have Microsoft SQL Server installed on the system.

Section 3.3 Database Setup

The Database Setup will install the component database and repositories. The repositories are shared folders that contain all of the Windows XP binaries. The component database contains information on all of the Windows XP Embedded components, including a reference to the repository in which the component's files reside, if the component has files associated with it.

Section 3.4 Installation Scenarios

These three installations can be divided into two scenarios: the single user scenario (Standalone) and the multi-user scenario (Client-Server). The development system minimum requirements are in Table 3.1. A faster CPU with more RAM is always more helpful.

The development system minimum requirements.

	Client	**Server**	**Standalone (local server)**
Software	Windows 2000 SP2 or later	Windows 2000 Server SP2 or later	Windows 2000 SP2 or later
CPU	500 MHz	500 MHz	500 MHz
RAM	128 MB	256 MB	256 MB
Disk space	200 MB	3 GB	3GB
Pagefile	300 MB	600 MB	600 MB

Table 3.1 Development System Minimum Requirements

In the single user scenario, all three installation steps are completed on a single computer (a standalone installation). This means that the development work is done using a single computer. The drawback to the Standalone installation is that performance can be affected by having the XP Embedded database, which stores all the component information, installed with the development tools on the same machine. The requirements in Table 3.1 will work, but a machine that has at minimum a 1 GHz CPU and 256 MB of RAM is highly recommended. Another drawback is that the database cannot be shared with other users.

Note: Because the exercises in this book involve creating custom components and making modifications to the Windows XP Embedded Database, a Standalone installation is assumed.

However, you may run into a recurring error when you begin installation. The following section is designed to provide a work-around if you encounter the same error. When executing a standalone installation, the Windows XP Embedded development kit installer performs the three-step installation process in a given order. When Windows XP Embedded was released, a standalone installation of the development kit occasionally resulted in an error: "The instance name specified is invalid."

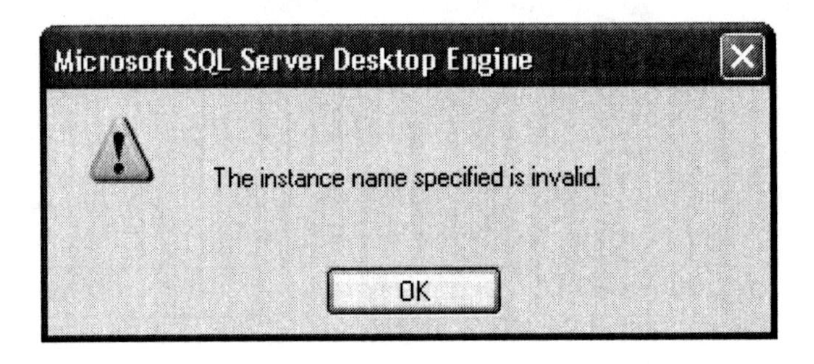

Figure 3.2 Error Notification

This is a legitimate error, and is supposed to appear when an attempt is made to install Microsoft SQL Server on a machine that already has Microsoft SQL Server installed. If you have previously installed Microsoft SQL Server, you're supposed to skip the Database Engine Setup and proceed to the Database Setup. On occasion the error appears on machines that do not have SQL Server installed, and the Microsoft SQL Server Desktop Engine appears in the Add/Remove Programs Control Panel applet. Simply skipping to the Database Setup is not an option because it generates an error indicating that setup cannot continue without the SQL Server Desktop Engine installed.

To get around the problem, you simply need to swap the order of the three steps mentioned above. The first exercise explains exactly how this is done, and is a good way to familiarize yourself with the Database setup even if you do not get the same error.

Note: If you prefer, you can proceed with a standard installation by clicking the Getting Started button at the top of the install screen.

Section 3.5 EXERCISE 1A

Execute the Database Engine Setup

1. If they exist on the system, the **Windows XP Embedded Tools** and **Microsoft SQL Server Desktop Engine** programs will need to be removed. The **Add or Remove Programs** Control Panel applet can be used to see if these programs are present on your system, and it will enable you to remove them. Select **Control Panel** from the **Start** menu and double-click on the **Add or Remove Programs** Control Panel applet. If **Windows XP Embedded Tools** and/or **Microsoft SQL Server Desktop Engine** appear in the list, they can be removed one at a time. Skip this step if neither of them shows up in the list. To individually remove a program, click on the program and then click the **Remove** button. Close the **Add or Remove Programs** Control Panel applet and the **Control Panel** when done.

2. Re-insert the Windows XP Embedded CD.

3. Click on **Database Engine Setup** when the setup screen appears. The Database Engine will install itself without prompting for any user input.

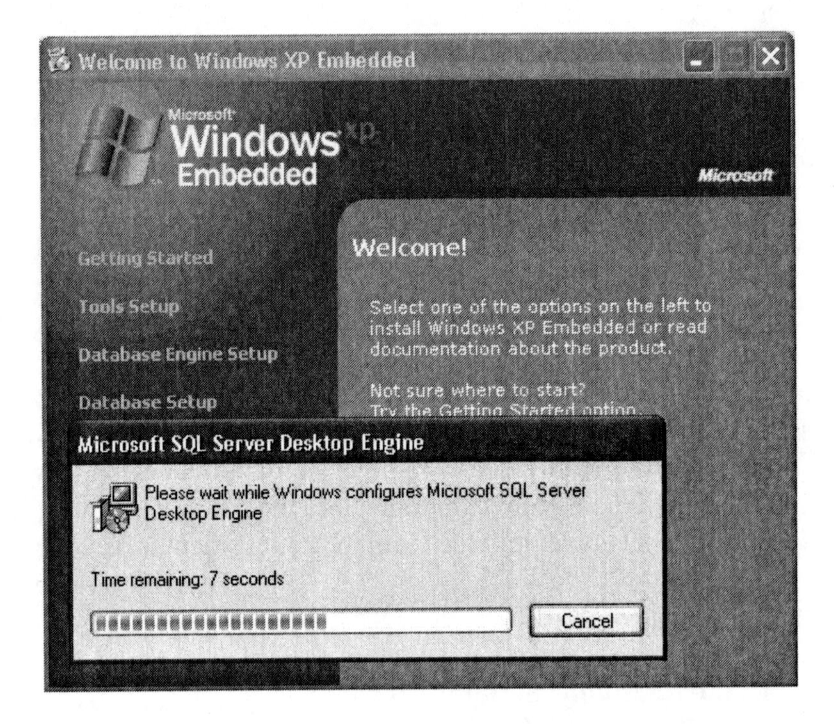

Figure 3.3 The Database Engine Setup install.

4. When the Desktop Engine Setup install is complete, reboot the system.

Execute the Database Setup

1. Re-insert the Windows XP Embedded CD after the system is booted up, then select **Database Setup**.

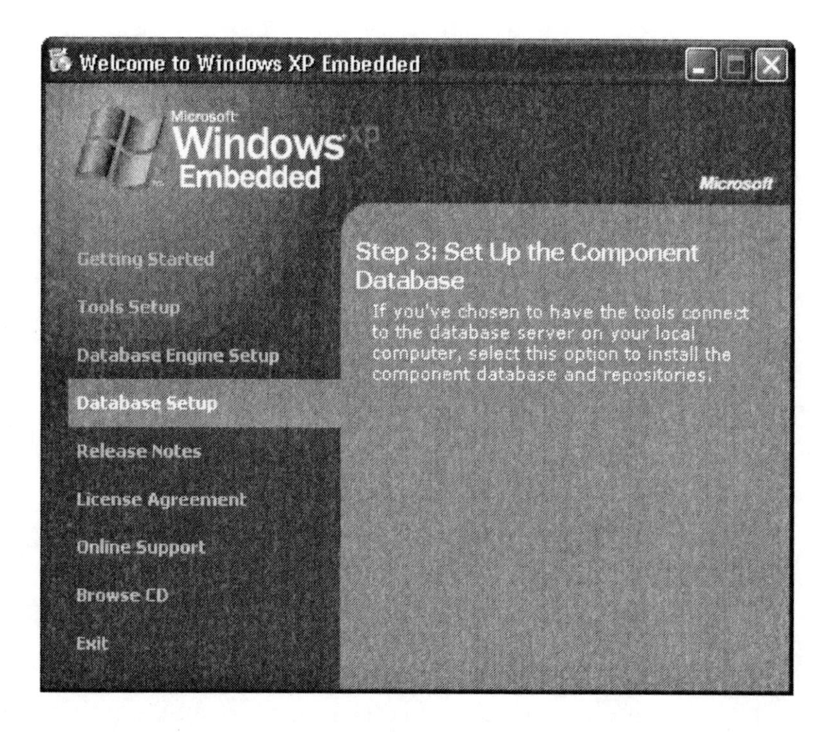

Figure 3.4 Select **Database Setup** following the Database Engine Setup and system reboot.

2. Right away you will be asked if you would like the system to attempt to change an MSDE/SQL Server configuration setting in order for the database to be installed. Select **Yes**, then click the **Next** button to continue.

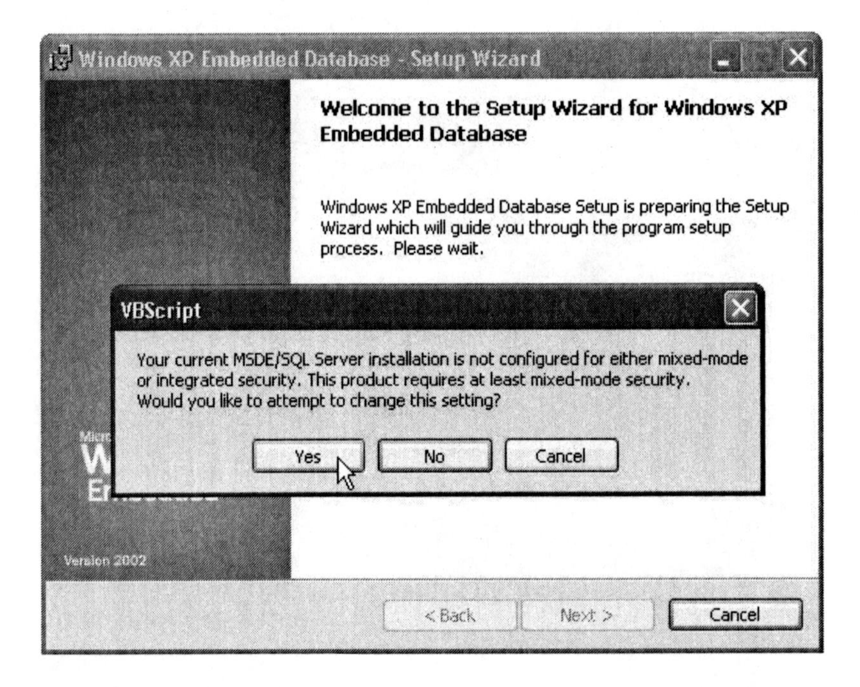

Figure 3.5 User interaction required during Database Setup. Select **Yes**.

3. The next couple of screens are typical and fairly straightforward: agreeing to the EULA, entering the user name, organization and CD product key (located on the CD sleeve).

4. The screen that follows the customer information/product key screen will ask which type of setup you wish to use to install. Select **Custom**.

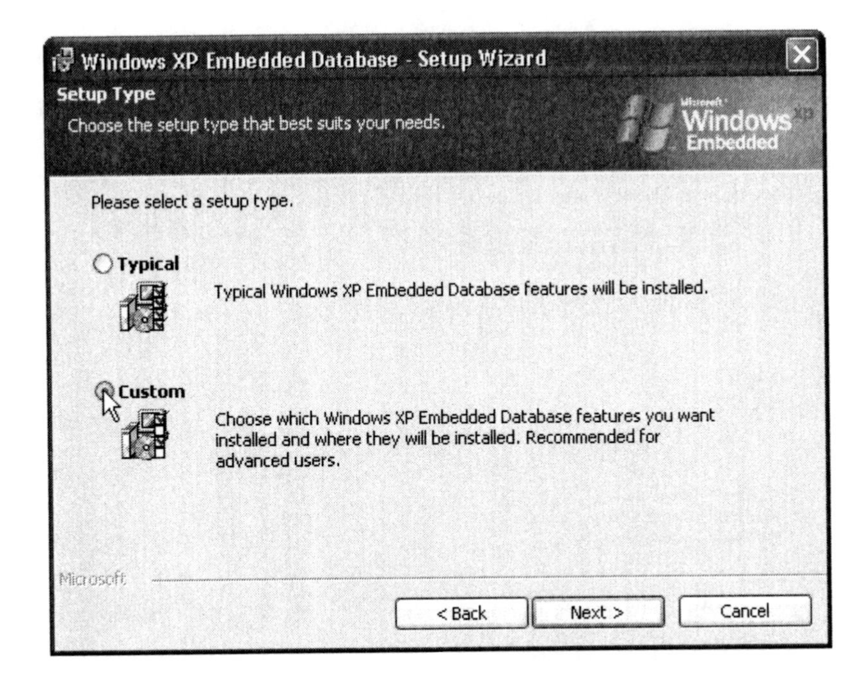

Figure 3.6 The Setup Type screen in the Database Setup install wizard.

5. The point of choosing the Custom Setup Type is to ensure that the database is being installed where you want it. Click the **Next** button when you are satisfied with the location of the database install.

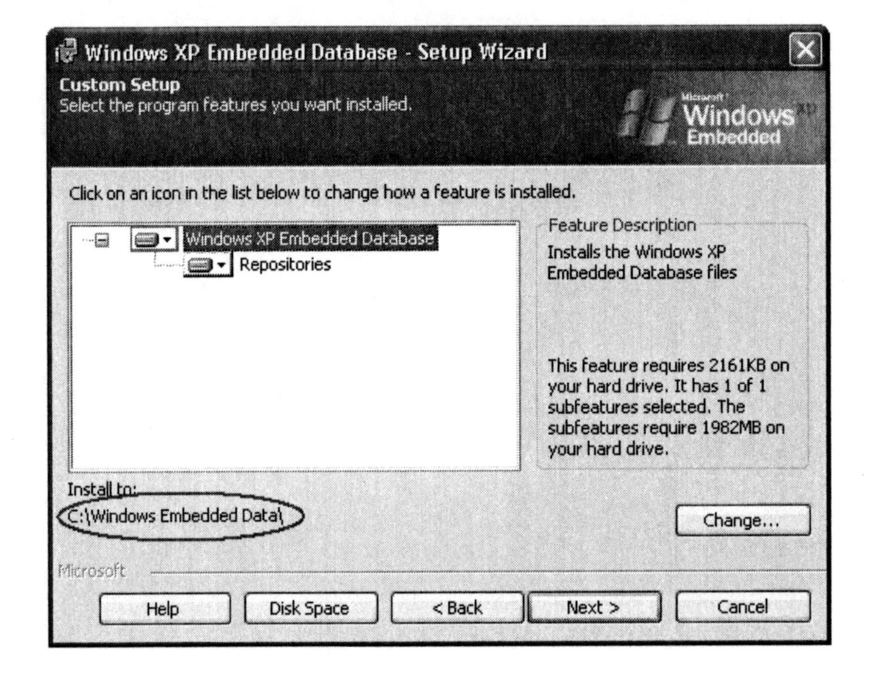

Figure 3.7 Make sure the database is installed where you want it.

6. Click the **Install** button on the screen that follows the Custom Setup screen and the database will install and expand itself. This may take several minutes.

7. The prompt that follows is basically a message which informs you that the installer will be installing a shared folder onto your system. Click the **Yes** button to continue the database installation.

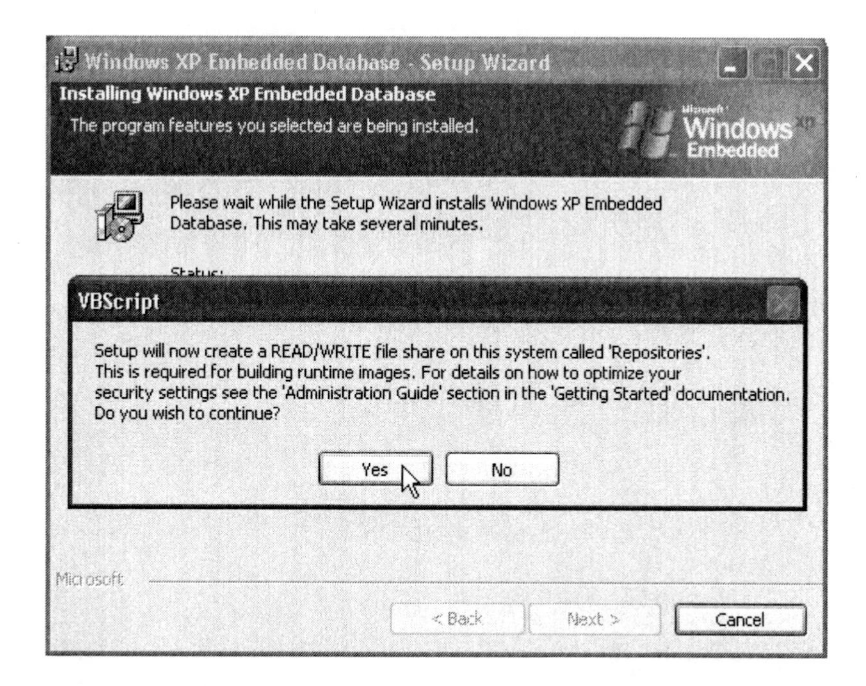

Figure 3.8 Prompt regarding the installation of a shared directory on your system.

8. It will take a number of minutes to copy the files and expand the database. After the database has finished installing, click the **Finish** button and then reboot the system.

Execute the Tools Setup

1. Re-insert the Windows XP Embedded CD, then select **Tools Setup**.

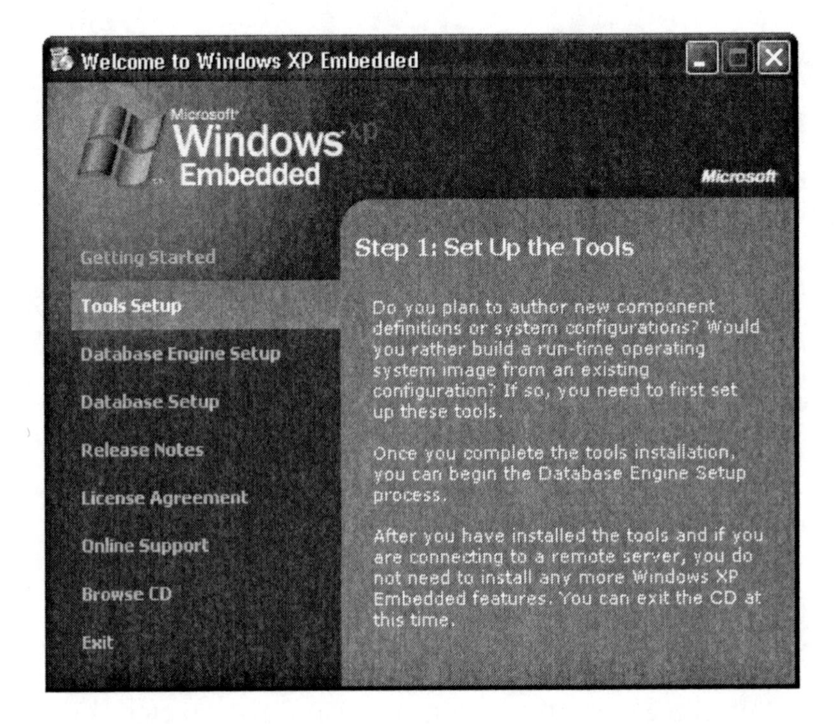

Figure 3.9 The Tools Setup step is the final step of the installation procedure.

2. Click the **Next** button on the first screen of the Tool Setup install wizard to start the installation process.

3. As with the Database Setup, the next couple of screens that follow prompt the user to agree to the EULA, enter the user name, organization and CD product key (located on the CD sleeve). Click the **Next** button to continue after the appropriate information has been entered.

4. The next screen is also similar to the Database Setup. Again, select **Custom** then click the **Next** button.

5. Once again, the main purpose of selecting the Custom Setup Type is so that you can make sure that the files, for the development tools in this case, are

being installed to the desired location. It also allows you to view what is being installed on your system.

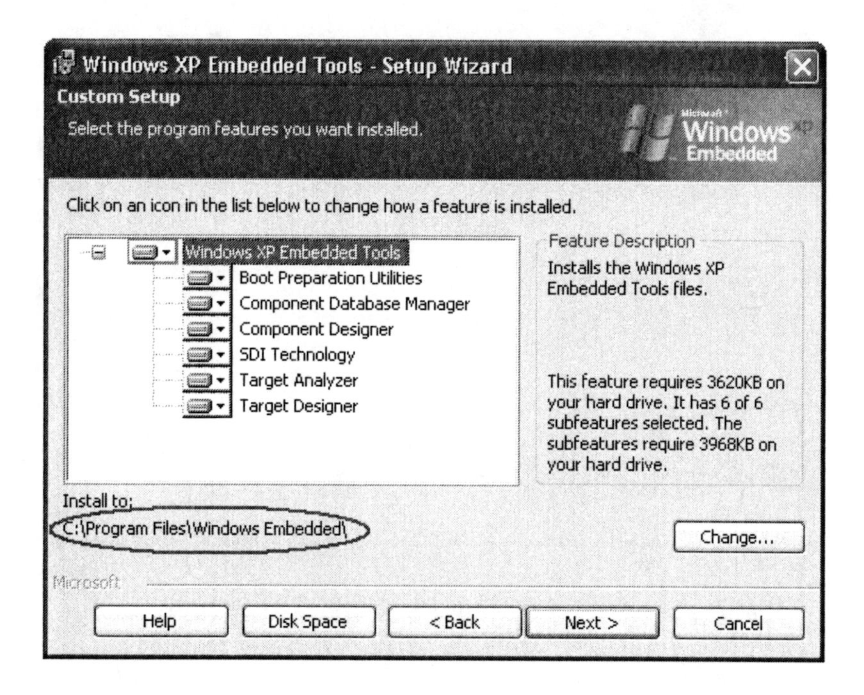

Figure 3.10 In the Custom Setup screen, make sure that the tools are being installed where you want them.

6. The next screen (Figure 3.11 below) is where you tell the system which computer you will be using as the Windows Embedded Server. Because the Database Engine Setup and Database Setup have already been done on the local machine, we will go with the default selection of specifying **This Computer** as the Windows Embedded Server. However, if the component database resides on another machine, you would select **A different computer** and then specify the name of the server which contains the component database. The **Destination folder for build process output** default setting can either be changed on this screen or it can be changed later from Target Designer. Click the **Next** button to continue with the Tools Setup.

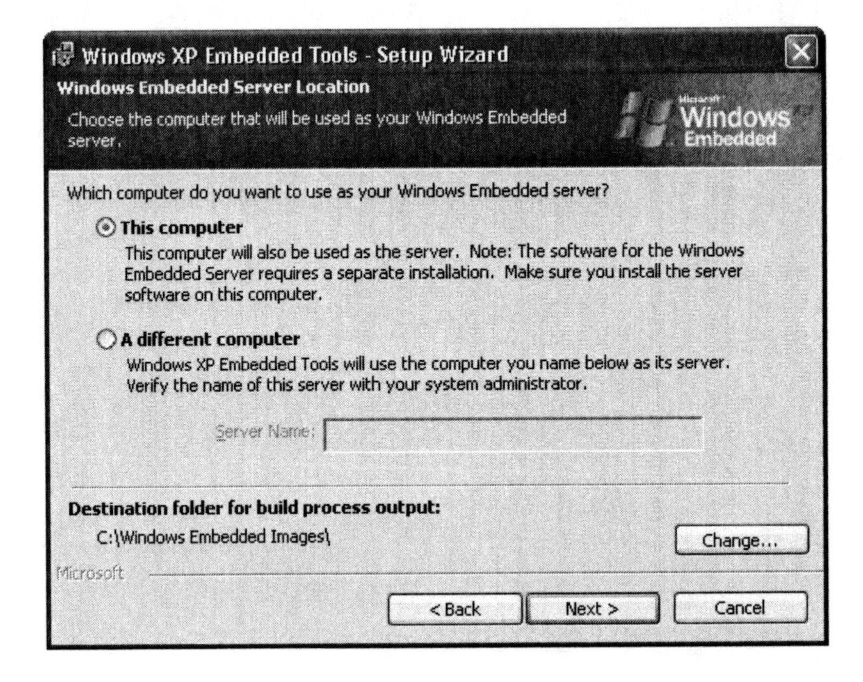

Figure 3.11 Windows Embedded Server Location screen

7. Click the **Install** button to complete the last portion of the Tools Setup.

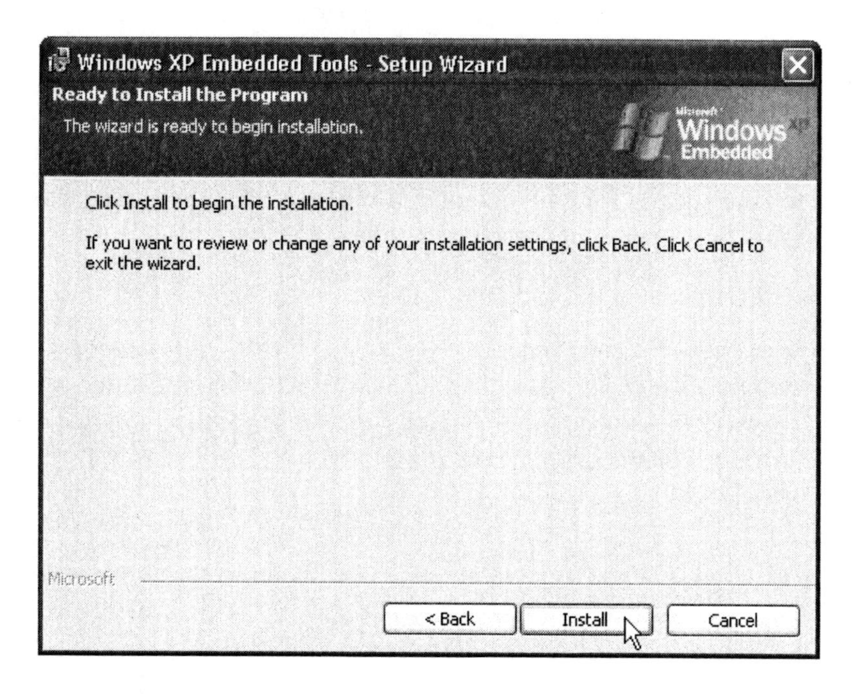

Figure 3.12 The last step prior to installing the tools.

8. After clicking the **Finish** button on the final screen of the Tools Setup, reboot the system one more time.

9. The installation of the Windows Embedded Studio development kit is now complete. As a quick test to make sure that everything installed correctly, open Target Designer. From the **Start** menu, click **Programs**, then **Windows Embedded Studio**, and then **Target Designer**. If Target Designer opens without any error or warning messages, then you will know that everything has installed correctly.

The multi-user scenario involves installing the XP Embedded database on a server, which should have Microsoft SQL Server installed on it. The advantage of having the database installed on its own dedicated computer is that the database can be shared by many users, and it will increase performance. Every user will have to install the development tools on his or her machine.

The next exercise comes directly from the XP Embedded help system and will not go into a lot of detail about SQL Server. The instructions are straightforward and are provided here simply for convenience. It will provide some guidance to help system administrators set up a shared component database (server setup). For further help, refer to Windows SQL Server 2000 Help.

Note: The Windows XP Embedded database can be installed on a server as well as on the standalone system. The next chapter will have an exercise which demonstrates how to switch between them, but the following exercise can be skipped if you only want to use a standalone installation.

Section 3.6 EXERCISE 1B

Install SQL Server 2000

Microsoft SQL Server 2000 is not included in the Windows XP Embedded installation media. There are various editions available, each with its own environments that are tailored to different work models. The component database will work on any of the editions. Choose the edition you want based on your requirements. SQL Server 2000 should be installed on Windows 2000 Server.

Set the authentication mode

SQL Server 2000 provides two methods for authenticating logins: Windows Authentication and SQL Server Authentication. **Windows XP Embedded requires Windows Authentication.** SQL Server supports mixed-mode authentication, which allows both for both methods. If it is set for SQL Server only, the database installation may prompt you to change to the required authentication mode.

1. Start SQL Server Enterprise Manager from the **Start** menu.

2. Expand the **Microsoft SQL Servers** node, and then expand the **SQL Server Group** node. Your database server registration is located below this node.

3. Right-click the ***<database server registration>*** node, and then click on **Properties**.

4. In the **SQL Server Properties** dialog box, select the **Security** tab. The current authentication mode is displayed in the **Security** group box.

5. Choose **SQL Server and Windows**, and click the **OK** button.

Set up user accounts

In addition to logging into their development systems using a network domain user account, developers connecting to a shared component database need to log on to the SQL Server database with a SQL Server login ID. They will also need to access the component database with a SQL Server user ID.

When developers use a network domain user account to log on to a development environment in situations where the database server is located on a different system than the Windows Embedded Studio tools, their cached credentials will be used to connect to the SQL Server database.

If the database server is not a member of a network domain, you need to create a matching user account on the SQL Server system for each user that needs to connect to the database. Use the same user name and password as the user account for the Windows Embedded Studio development system.

The system administrator who installs the database and the component database engine holds all the permissions in the database. Any other user requiring access to the component database must have a SQL Server user account. You can create a SQL Server user account using Enterprise Manager. To create a SQL Server user account, you need to create a SQL Server login ID and a SQL Server user ID.

To create a SQL Server login ID:

1. Start SQL Server Enterprise Manager from the **Start** menu.

2. Expand the **Microsoft SQL Servers** node, and then expand the **SQL Server Group** node. Your database server registration is located below this node.

3. Expand the ***<database server registration>*** node, and then expand the **Security** folder.

4. Double-click the **Logins** icon, and then choose **New Login** from the **Action** menu.

5. In the **SQL Server Login Properties – New Login** dialog box, type the user name in the **Name** box using the ***<domain\Name>*** format. Make sure that the **Windows Authentication** radio button is selected.

6. Click on the **Ok** button.

To create a SQL Server user ID:

1. Start SQL Server Enterprise manager from the **Start** menu.

2. Expand the **Microsoft SQL Servers** node, and then expand the **SQL Server Group** node. Your database server registration is located below this node.

3. Expand the ***<database server registration>*** node, and then expand the **Databases** folder.

4. Expand the **MantisSQLDB** folder, and then open the **Users** icon.

5. Choose **New Database User** from the **Action** menu.

6. In the **Database User Properties – New User** dialog box, select the user you want to add from the **Login name** list. By default, the **User name** box is populated with the same information.

7. Choose the permissions for the user by selecting the appropriate database roles in the **Database role membership**. The following table shows the pre-defined database roles exposed in the Windows XP Embedded component database and you can assign any one of these to a user:

Role	Description
WES_Reader	Members have read-only access to the component database.
WES_Importer	Members have change and read access to the component database.
WES_Admin	Members have full access to the repositories share and can delete from the component database.

Table 3.2 Database Roles

8. Click the **Ok** button.

Install the tools on the client-development system(s)

The same procedure from the section titled ***Execute the Tools Setup*** in Exercise 1A can be used to install the tools in each client machine. The main difference in installing the tools on a standalone system is that you will select **A different com-**

puter to specify the computer you want to use as your Windows Embedded server, and you will enter the name of the server in the **Server Name** box.

The next chapter will focus on the Component Database Manager. The Component Database Manager will be used to test the installation that was just completed (either Exercise 1A or 1B), explore the capabilities of the Component Database Manager, and update the component database with Microsoft's latest updates, which will be download from the embedded MSDN web site.

CHAPTER 4 Component Database Manager

Windows Embedded Studio includes the Component Database Manager, which provides management functions for the component database and repositories. Both the Component Designer and Target Designer tools use the component database and repositories. The Component Database Manager can be used to:

- Import component (SLD) files, which are created by Component Designer and contain database objects.
- Remove database objects.
- Specify or change the XP Embedded SQL database source that Target Designer and Component Designer will use.
- Manage the repository locations which contain files that must be copied into the XP Embedded operating system when built by Target Designer.

Component Database Manager can be launched from Target Designer or Component Designer, or it can be opened manually from the **Start** menu. It will be opened in one of the two modes of operation: *read import mode* or *exclusive mode*, depending on permissions granted and whether or not there are others active users.

In read import mode you can view database contents and import database objects, but you cannot delete objects or modify database objects or properties. If the database is being used by another user or program Component Database Manager will open in read import mode by default. For example, if another user has Component Database Manager open on a shared database, or if Target Designer or Component Designer is open on a standalone system, Component Database Manager will open in read import mode and a message will pop up to inform you of it.

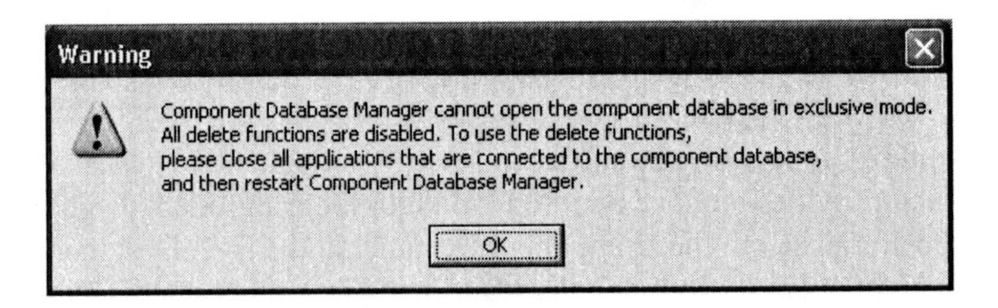

Figure 4.1 Warning if an attempt is made to open Component Database Manager while another user or program is using the database.

Component Database Manager will be in exclusive mode if it is launched from the **Start** menu and nothing else is using the database. Exclusive mode enables you to make changes to the database, including object deletions. All other tools are blocked from using the database when in exclusive mode.

Section 4.1 The Database Tab

When you launch Component Database Manager, the **Database** tab is displayed. The **Database** tab displays the location of the currently selected component database server location and provides the function to change this setting. You can also import component definition (SLD) files into the component database from this tab. A later exercise will demonstrate this process.

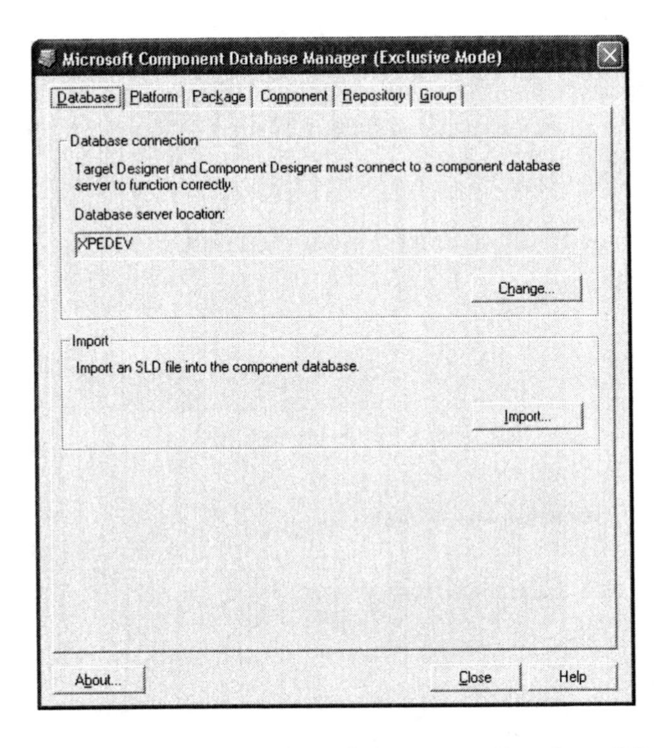

Figure 4.2 The Database tab of Component Database Manager.

The exercise will also test whether or not the development kit was installed correctly. Component Database Manager should open in exclusive mode without errors or warnings. The next exercise will demonstrate how to change the component database server location to work with Target Designer and Component Designer. If Component Database Manager fails to connect to the database, only the **Database** tab will be present. Refer to the installation troubleshooting section of the Windows XP Embedded Platform help for assistance. If you cannot connect to your shared database on a server, consult with your system administrator.

Section 4.2 EXERCISE 2

Change the database server location

1. Launch Component Database Manager from the **Start** menu. It can be found in the **Windows Embedded Studio** menu by clicking **Start**, then **All Programs**.

2. Click the **Change** button and the **Change Database Server Location** dialog will appear.

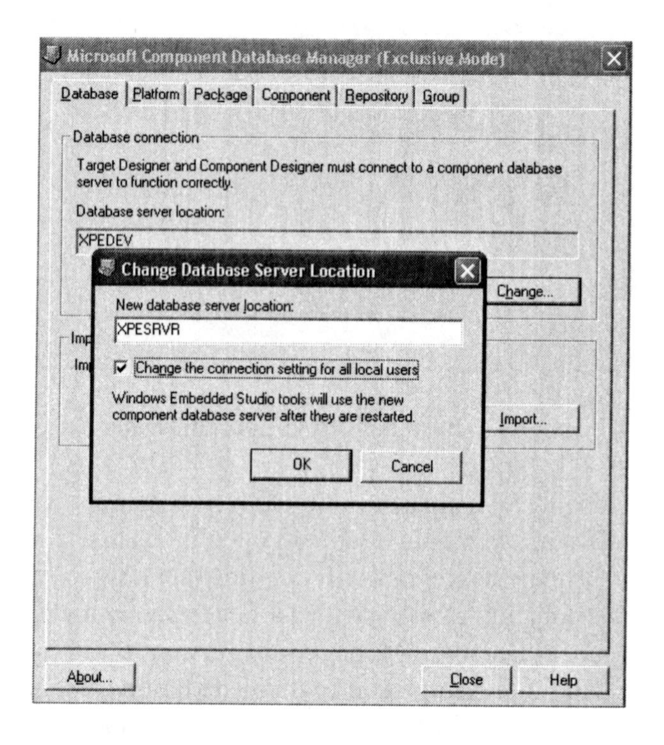

Figure 4.3 Changing the database server location.

3. Enter the name of the component database server machine that you wish to use. If a component database is not set up on a server, press the **Cancel** but-

ton. If you want all users of the local machine to use the new database server machine, check the check box under the server name you just entered. Click the **OK** button when finished.

4. If Component Database Manager cannot connect to the database server you specify, an error dialog will appear, followed by another dialog which will give you the option of keeping the new setting or reverting to the old setting.

5. When asked to confirm New Server location, click **Yes**.

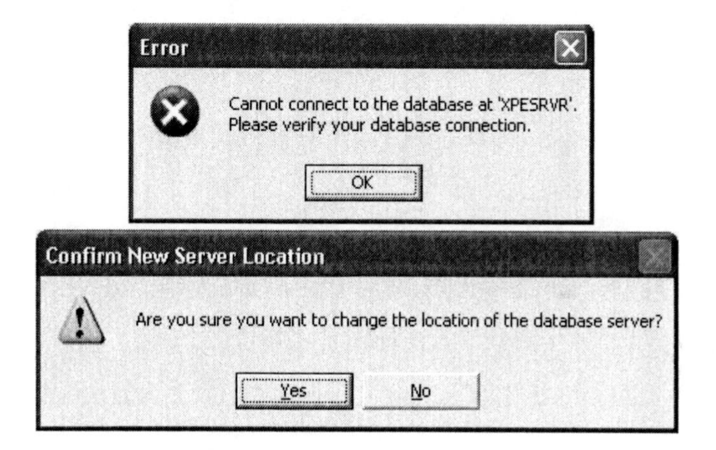

Figure 4.4 If unable to connect to the specified server, after clicking **OK** on the error message dialog, you will have the option to keep the new setting or revert to the old one.

With Component Database Manager still open, the next section will describe each of the remaining tabs and define some terms associated with XP Embedded. How everything comes together will become a little more clear once we begin working with Component Designer.

Section 4.3 The Platform Tab

.

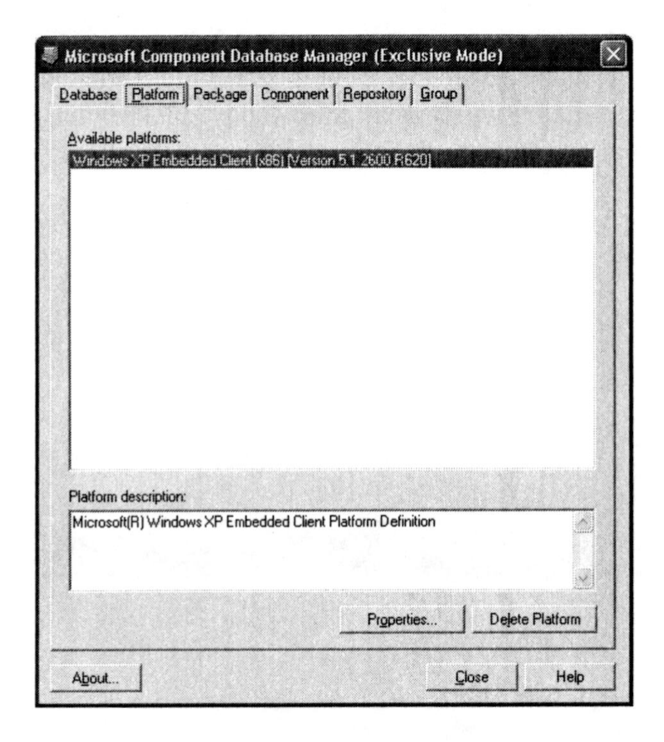

Figure 4.5 The Platform tab of Component Database Manager

The **Platform** tab contains a list of all the available platforms for developing an XP Embedded run-time image. The platform identifies the operating system on which the run-time image is based, along with the components, resources, and repositories associated with it. Currently Windows XP Embedded only supports the x86 platform, thus it is the only platform on the list.

Section 4.4 The Package Tab

Components and/or repositories can be grouped together in a package for Component Database Manager to use.

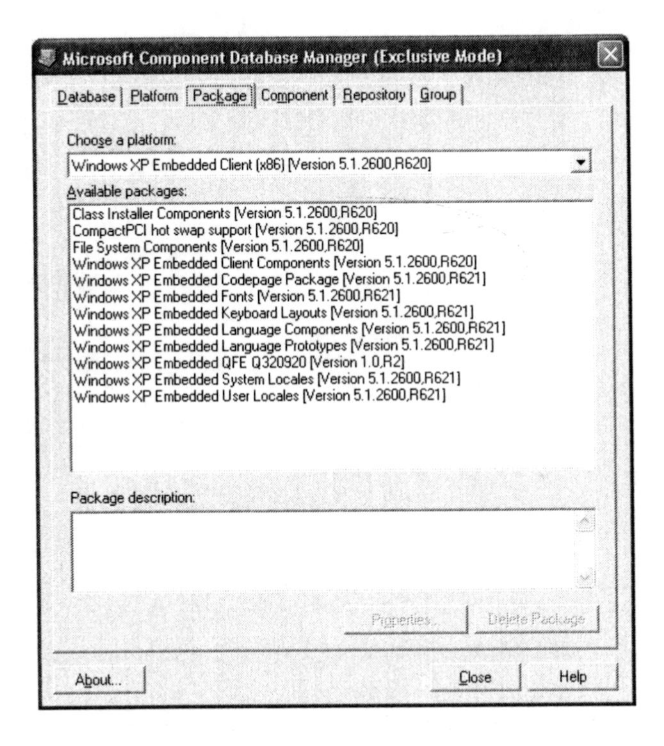

Figure 4.6 The Package tab of Component Database Manager.

A package is associated with a particular platform. All of the available packages for a specific platform can be viewed, and deleted, on the **Package** tab of Component Database Manager. Packages enable you to manage multiple components or repositories as one. For example, you can remove all components that belong to a package from the database by removing the package through the **Package** tab. Packages will be covered in further detail under the subject of Component Designer.

Section 4.5 The Component Tab

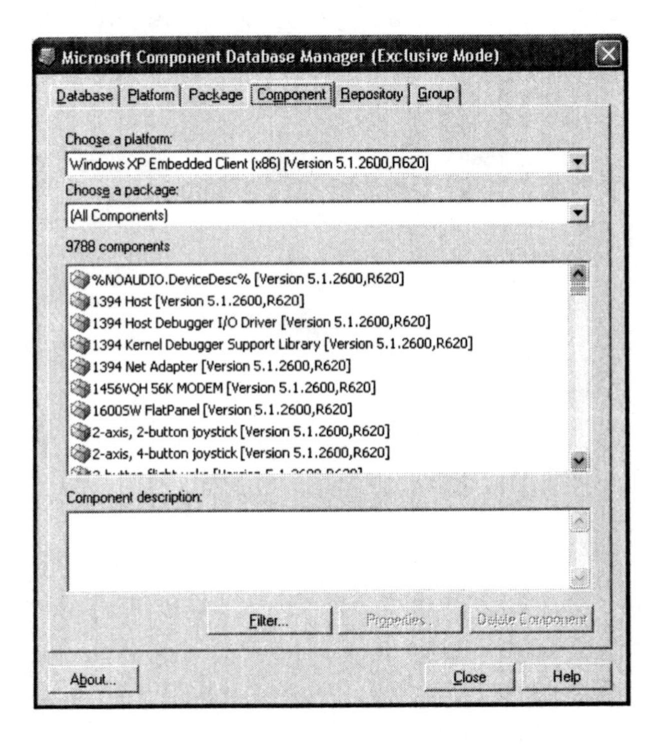

Figure 4.7 The Component tab of Component Database Manager.

Components contain all the necessary information for the development tools to incorporate their specific functionality into the operating system. For example, a driver component can include the resources needed for it to be built into the run-time image and loaded by the operating system. A component is the smallest individually selectable piece of functionality that can be included or excluded from a run-time image, and is made up of a combination of files, registry entries, and dependencies. More details about components will be covered under the topic of Component Designer. On the **Component** tab, you can view a list of components, view a selected component's properties, or delete a selected component. Only one component at a time can be deleted from the database on the **Component** tab. By default, all components that are associated with the x86 platform are listed on the

Component tab. However, you can also list all components that are part of a particular package.

Section 4.5.1 Filter Tool

In addition, the component list can be put through a custom filter, created using the Filter Manager, in which only components that comply with the assigned filter rules are listed. A filter consists of a name, a combination of one or more rules, and a filter description. The name that you assign to your filter is used to identify the filter and it should reflect the purpose of the filter. Each filter needs to include at least one rule. The following list of predefined rules can be combined using the **AND** and **OR** logical operators:

- Component display name contains [substring]
- Component description contains [substring]
- Component vendor name contains [substring]
- Component version string contains [substring]
- Component is configurable by the user
- Component can be included in the same configuration multiple times
- Component contains the following file: [filelist]
- Component belongs to the following package: [package]
- Component belongs to ANY of the following categories: [categories]

In the next exercise, you will be introduced to the Filter Manager. The Filter Manager enables you to create modify, delete, or apply component filters. The Filter

Manager can be launched and utilized not only in Component Database Manager, but in Target Designer and Component Designer as well. Even though the Filter Manager can only be launched from any one of these three tools, it operates the same and all the filters will be available regardless of which tool is used to launch it.

Section 4.6 EXERCISE 3

Create a filter to list all Control Panel components

1. Launch Component Database Manager from **Start\All Programs**, then click the **Component** tab.

2. Open the Filter Manager by clicking the **Filter** button near the bottom of the **Component** tab.

3. Click the **New** button in the Filter Manager.

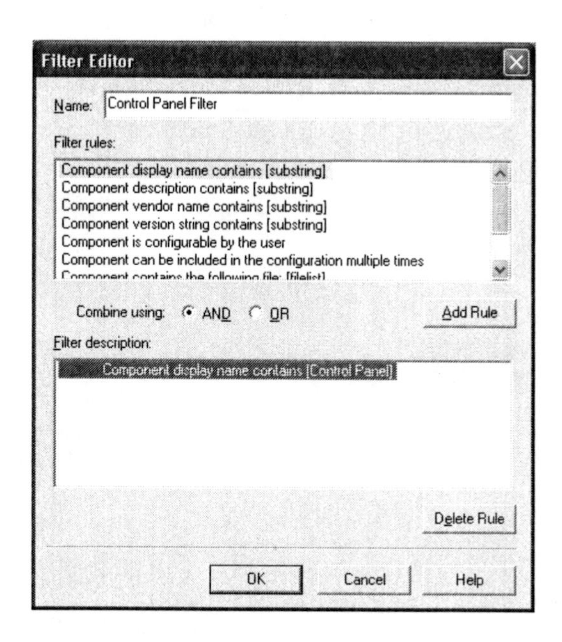

Figure 4.8 The Filter Editor dialog appears as a result of clicking the **New** button on the Filter Manager.

4. In the **Name** field, type Control Panel Filter.

5. In **Filter rules**, click on **Component display name contains [substring]**, then click the **Add Rule** button.

6. Double-click the filter rule that was just added to the **Filter description**, then enter the substring for which we wish to search – in this case Control Panel. Click the **OK** button to close the Filter Editor.

Note: To create a more thorough filter that will include any components that contain Control Panel Extension files (.cpl), you could click the ***OR*** *radio button and add the rule* ***Component contains the following file:[.cpl]****. However, including a file list filter rule can sometimes take up a significant amount of time. For this exercise, the component display name rule is sufficient to demonstrate the capability of filters.*

7. The newly created filter is now available for use. The filter can be applied immediately by clicking the **Apply Filter** button in the Filter Manager, or it can be applied at any other time by selecting the filter from the **Choose a package** pull-down menu in Component Database Manager. Target Designer and Component Designer also provide pull-down menus to select any available filters. Highlight Control Panel Filter in the filter list and click **Apply Filter** now.

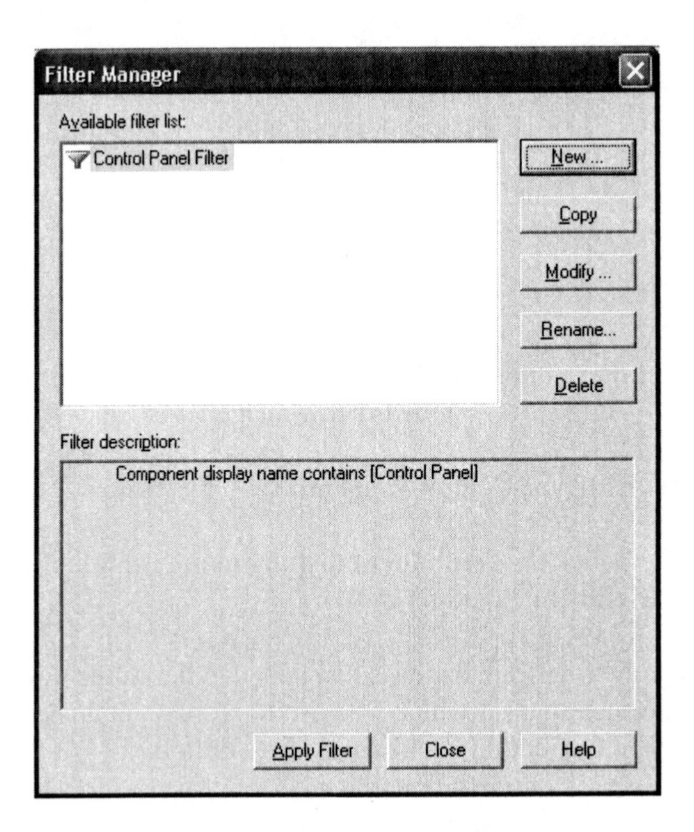

Figure 4.9 The Filter Manager displays all available filters, and any one of them can be applied from the Filter Manager.

Note that the only components that are listed are the ones whose name contains the substring "Control Panel". All the components can be listed by selecting **All Components** from the **Choose a package** pull-down menu.

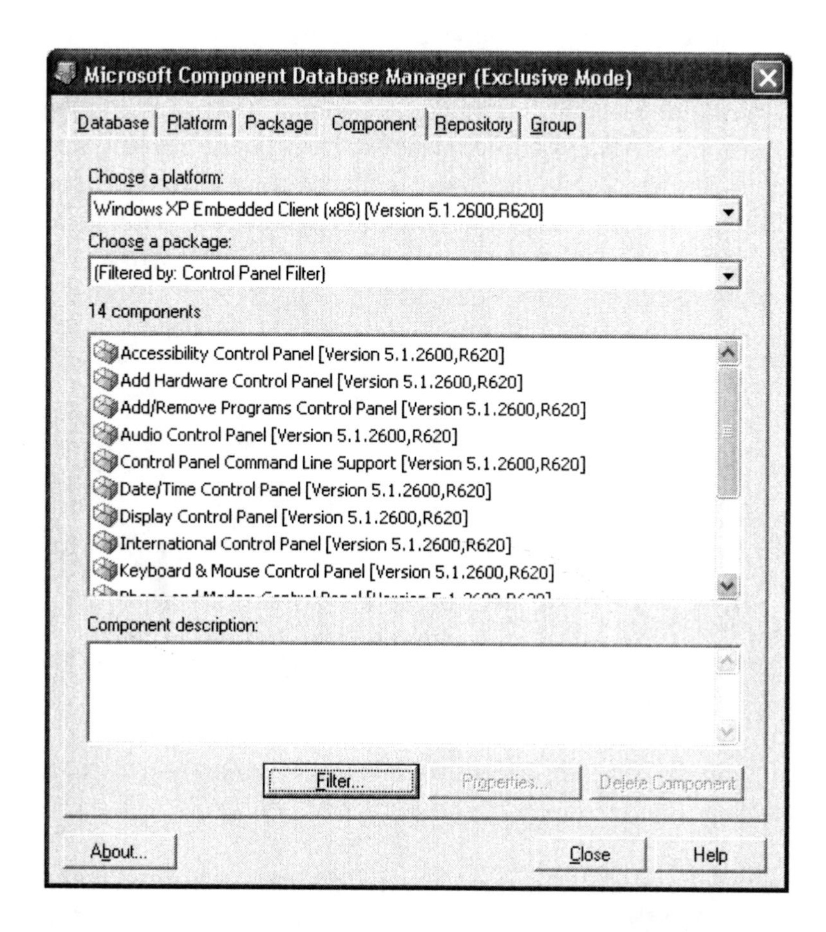

Figure 4.10 The results of applying the Control Panel Filter.

Section 4.7 Windows XP Embedded Updates

The Microsoft Embedded MSDN web site contains a great deal of useful information, including links to newsgroups and downloads. In the next exercise, you will download the latest XP Embedded updates from the Embedded MSDN web site, then install them into the database using Component Database Manager. The downloaded files will be self-extracting executables. Almost all of them consist of component definition files (SLD) with repositories. These SLD files are imported into the component database in the same manner that you would import your own custom SLD files into the database, which you will be doing later on when you create a component using Component Designer. For now we will not be concerned with what is in the SLD files. Installing all the updates is not required, but it is recommended.

Section 4.8 EXERCISE 4

Download the latest Windows XP Embedded updates from the Embedded MSDN web site

1. Launch a web browser and enter the web address http://msdn.microsoft.com/embedded.

2. In the left pane, expand the **Windows XP Embedded** node, then click **Downloads**.

3. Under the **Windows Development\Embedded Development** node, expand the **Windows XP Embedded** node. Here you will find a folder, **QFEs**, which contains the latest Windows XP Embedded updates. There is also another folder that contains the **Multilingual User Interface Language Packs**, which allow users to switch the User Interface in XP Embedded from one language to another.

Note: The procedure for almost all of the XP Embedded downloads is the same. For this exercise, we will download and install the first one, but the procedure from this step onward can be repeated for the remaining QFEs and/or Multilingual User Interface Language Packs that come in the form of a self-extracting executable consisting of SLD files and repositories.

4. Expand the **QFEs** node and click on the first update link, **26 June 2002 Cumulative Patch for Windows Media Player for Windows XP Embedded**.

5. Read the entire page. It includes a link to the Knowledge Base Article which contains more details about the update that you are about to download and install. When you are finished reading the page and/or Knowledge Base Article, you can close the Knowledge Base Article window and click on the **download** link. First you will be prompted to read and agree with the license agreement. If you agree with the license agreement by clicking the **Yes** button, you will then be prompted to open or save the self-extracting executable file, **Q320920.exe**

6. Save it to a folder on your system. Browse to the folder where you saved the executable, and extract the files. Typically, the updates will contain at least one SLD file and a repository folder, which contains the file, or files, that come with the component or components included in the update. Some updates have more than one SLD file and/or repository folder, and some come with documentation for the update.

Importing the Updates

1. Launch Component Database Manager from **Start\All Programs**, then click the **Import** button on the **Database** tab.

2. Click the browse button (…) and browse to the folder which contains the SLD file. Select the SLD file once you find it and click the **Open** button.

3. Make sure that the Repository Root indicates the computer that you wish to import the SLD file onto. Also make sure that the checkbox labeled **Copy repository files to repository root** is checked, then click the **Import** button.

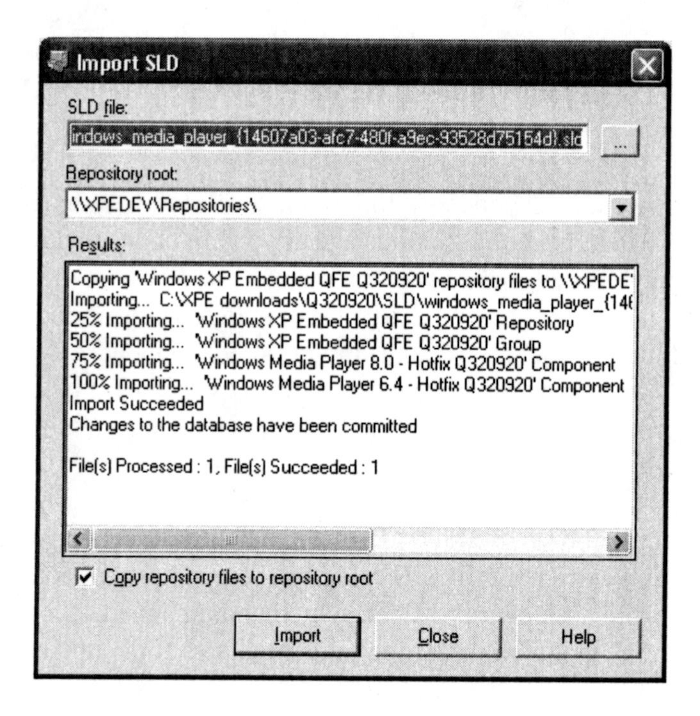

Figure 4.10 The Import SLD dialog after a successful import of an SLD file.

4. If you have downloaded all of the updates and wish to install all of them now, you can repeat the procedure to install each one of them by selecting each SLD file using the browse feature and clicking the **Import** button. You do not have to close the **Import SLD** dialog each time you import a SLD file. Click the **Close** button after you are finished importing SLD files.

5. You can verify that the component was imported by selecting the **Component** tab in Component Database Manager and finding the newly imported component. To help you find the update component, you can click the **Filter**

button and use the Filter Manager to create a filter that will display all components whose name contains the substring "Q320920".

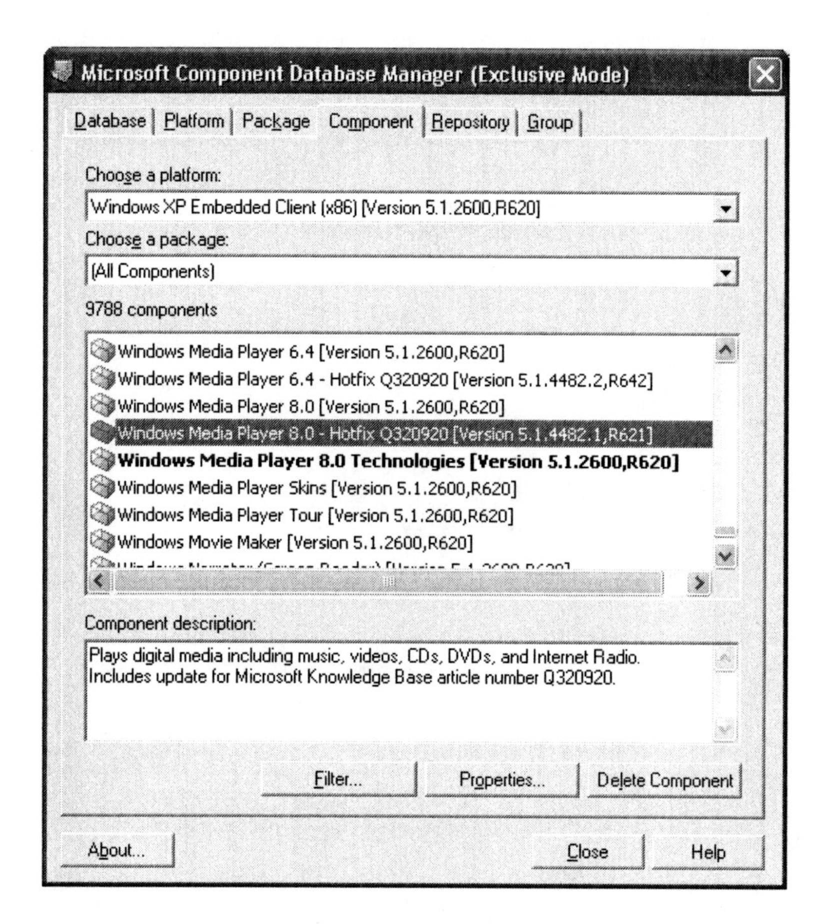

Figure 4.11 The **Component** tab displays the components that exist in the database.

6. You can verify that the component's repository was created by selecting the **Repository** tab in Component Database Manager. You can also open **My Computer** and browse to the location of the newly created repository to verify that the binaries were copied.

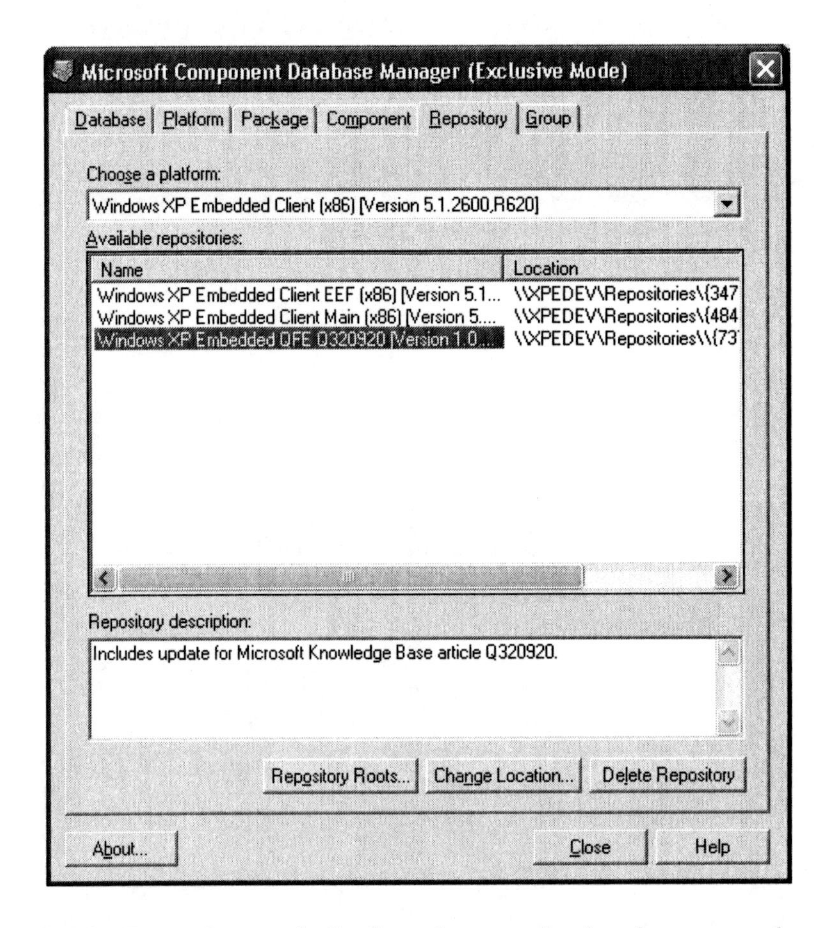

Figure 4.12 The **Repository** tab displays the repositories that are on the specified component database server.

7. Click the **Close** button to complete the exercise.

The remaining tabs, the **Repository** tab and the **Group** tab require a better knowledge of components before they can be completely understood. The topics of repositories and groups will be covered in the Component Designer chapter. Before learning how to build custom components you will first need to learn how to gather hardware information on a target device and how to build a run-time image.

CHAPTER 5 *Target Analyzer*

In order to build a run-time image for your platform, you will have to know exactly which hardware exists so that you can include the necessary operating system specific components. These components include items such as the appropriate Hardware Abstraction Layer (HAL), or necessary device drivers, such as an IDE controller. It can be difficult to determine the exact architecture of a system by visual inspection or from a set of specification documents. Windows Embedded Studio includes a tool, Target Analyzer, to help determine the hardware components that exist on a target device.

Section 5.1 Overview

From the standpoint of the hardware-software interface, the exact architecture of a system can easily be determined. Target Analyzer collects a relatively small amount of data about the system and generates an output file. This output file can be used to create a base platform configuration or a macro component.

There are two versions of the program that can detect hardware on a target device: Target Analyzer (TA.EXE) and Target Analyzer Probe (TAP.EXE). Either version runs on a target system to analyze the hardware configuration of that platform and creates an Extensible Markup Language (XML) file, with the extension .pmq, that represents the configuration of the target hardware.

TA.EXE is a 16-bit application that is run from DOS. TAP.EXE is a protected Microsoft Win32 application that runs from Windows 2000 or Windows XP. It obtains information about Plug and Play devices detected by the host operating system (Windows 2000/XP). For this reason TAP.EXE can "see" more devices and thus provide a more detailed description of the hardware.

Device Type	TA.EXE	TAP.EXE
Plug and Play BIOS	1	1
PCI	1	1
ACPI	2	1
USB	2	1
1394	2	1
SCSI	2	1
PCMCIA	2	1
DiskOnChip	1	1
ISA	2	2
HAL	3	1
CPU	3	1
IDE	2	1
Software Enumerated Devices	4	1

Table 5.1 The difference between the two versions of Target Analyzer

1 = Detects presence and devices; 2 = Detects presence only; 3 = Best guess; 4 = Will not detect

From the table, it can be seen that TAP.EXE is able to detect more than TA.EXE. It may seem awkward or inconvenient to have to install Windows 2000 or XP just to use TAP.EXE, but there are advantages. In addition to getting more information about your target hardware by using TAP.EXE on the system, installing one of these two 32-bit desktop operating systems on the target device will prove that the Windows XP Embedded should run on the device. If the device's hard disk has two primary partitions (each large enough to store the operating systems), the system can be set up for dual booting and boot to either the Windows desktop OS on the first partition or XP Embedded on the second partition. This can be helpful during development when you may need to rebuild and deploy the image more than once in order to try out different configuration settings. On the other hand, for various reasons you might not able to install Windows 2000 or Windows XP on your system. It could be because of storage limitations or because of the lack of a CD ROM drive on the device. Or perhaps your goal is to create more of a minimal build. In that case, you would use TA.EXE. It may not detect as much as TAP.EXE, leaving more work for you to do, but it is still better than trying to piece together a Target Designer OS configuration from scratch. You will be required to know more about the hardware so that you can add the necessary components. Typical components that are required for the XP Embedded image to run are:

- IDE Controllers
- Memory Access Controllers
- PCI/ISA Bridges or Controllers
- Keyboard/Mouse Components
- Display Adapters

Since Windows XP Embedded requires the keyboard/mouse components and a display adapter, there are "Null" drivers for these components if you wish to have a headless system, but that will be discussed in further detail under the topic of Embedded Enabling Features.

Both versions of Target Analyzer run from the command prompt and the usage is not too complicated:

TA [/O *filename*] [/B] [/Q] [/?]

- or -

TAP [/O *filename*] [/R] [/Q] [/?]

Command	Description
/O *filename*	Specifies the output path and/or filename. The filename must have a .pmq extension. If no filename is specified, the default output filename is *devices.pmq*.
/B	(TA only) When it is known that BIOS ACPI support is incompatible with Windows XP or Windows 2000 SP2, or when hardware detection problems occur, this flag forces the detection of the target system hardware as a legacy computer system by disabling ACPI.
/R	(TAP only) Runs a reduced scan of registry path ControlSet001. By default, TAP scans the CurrentControlSet registry path.
/Q	Sets quiet mode to suppress all output during the hardware detection process.
/?	Displays the usage help text.

Table 5.2 Command Prompt Parameters

Section 5.2 EXERCISE 5

Use TA.EXE to detect target device hardware

1. Create a bootable floppy disk. In Windows XP Professional, this can be done by opening **My Computer**, then right-click on **3½ Floppy (A:)** and select **Format…** from the menu selection. When the dialog pops up, click the **Create an MS-DOS startup disk** check box so that a green check mark appears in the box, then click the **Start** button. If a dialog box appears warning you that all data on the disk will be lost, click the **OK** button. Click the **Close** button when the disk is done formatting.

Note: The Windows 2000 format command does not provide the ability to format a floppy disk as bootable, as described in this step. If you have the MS-DOS operating system, you can use the MS-DOS version of format.com to format a floppy disk as bootable with the command line ***format a: /s****. You can also use the MS-DOS command* ***sys a:*** *to make a non-bootable floppy disk into a bootable disk.*

2. Copy TA.EXE onto the floppy disk from the folder C:**\Program Files\Windows Embedded\utilities**.

3. With the floppy disk in the floppy disk drive, reboot the computer. The boot order in the BIOS settings needs to be set to allow the computer to attempt to boot from the floppy drive first. If the computer does not boot to DOS, reboot the system, enter the BIOS setup, and check the boot order setting.

4. Once the system has booted to DOS, type the following command at the command prompt:

   ta /o dev_ta.pmq

   Optionally, you can save the screen output of Target Analyzer to a text file (it might be helpful for debugging):

   ta /o dev_ta.pmq > ta_out.txt

Note: It is a good practice to give the PMQ file a name that reflects which version of Target Analyzer was used to create it.

5. Remove the floppy disk and reboot the computer to the desktop Windows OS (XP/2000).

6. Launch **My Computer** from the **Start** menu, and then create a new folder named **XPE dev** in the root directory of the development system. Inside **XPE dev**, create another new folder and name it **TA_DATA**

7. Copy the file **dev_ta.pmq** from the A: drive to the newly created folder C:**XPE dev\TA_DATA**. You will use XML Notepad to examine dev_ta.pmq, along with the resulting file produced from TAP.EXE after completing the next procedure.

Note: XML Notepad is a special version of Notepad used to edit XML files. It can be obtained from http://msdn.microsoft.com/library/default.asp?url=/library/en-us/dnxml/html/xmlpaddownload.asp.

Use TAP.EXE to detect target device hardware

1. Open a command window by selecting **Run...** from the **Start** menu and typing in **cmd.exe** in the text box.

2. Type the following line at the command prompt:

   cd \Program Files\Windows Embedded\utilities

3. Next, type:

   tap /o dev_tap.pmq

   As with TA.EXE, the Target Analyzer screen output can be captured by typing:

   tap /o dev_tap.pmq > tap_out.txt

4. Launch **My Computer** and browse to the folder C:**Program Files\Windows Embedded\utilities**.

5. Copy the file **dev_tap.pmq** to the folder C:\ **XPE dev\TA_DATA**.

Examine the contents of dev_ta.pmq and dev_tap.pmq using XML Notepad

1. Browse to the folder C:**Program Files\Windows Embedded\dtd**.

2. Copy the two files, **devices.dtd** and **Mantis.dtd** to the folder C:\ **XPE dev\TA_DATA**.

Note: If you are copying the files by using the mouse to select then drag the two files to the desktop folder, make sure you use the right mouse button to drag the files so that you can make sure the files get copied and not moved.

Without going into the details of XML, a DTD, or Document Type Definition, describes an XML document. The two DTD files need to reside in the same directory as the PMQ files in order for XML Notepad to be able to read the PMQ files.

3. Launch **XML Notepad** from the **Start** menu and open **dev_ta.pmq**, which is located in the folder C:\ **XPE dev\TA_DATA**.

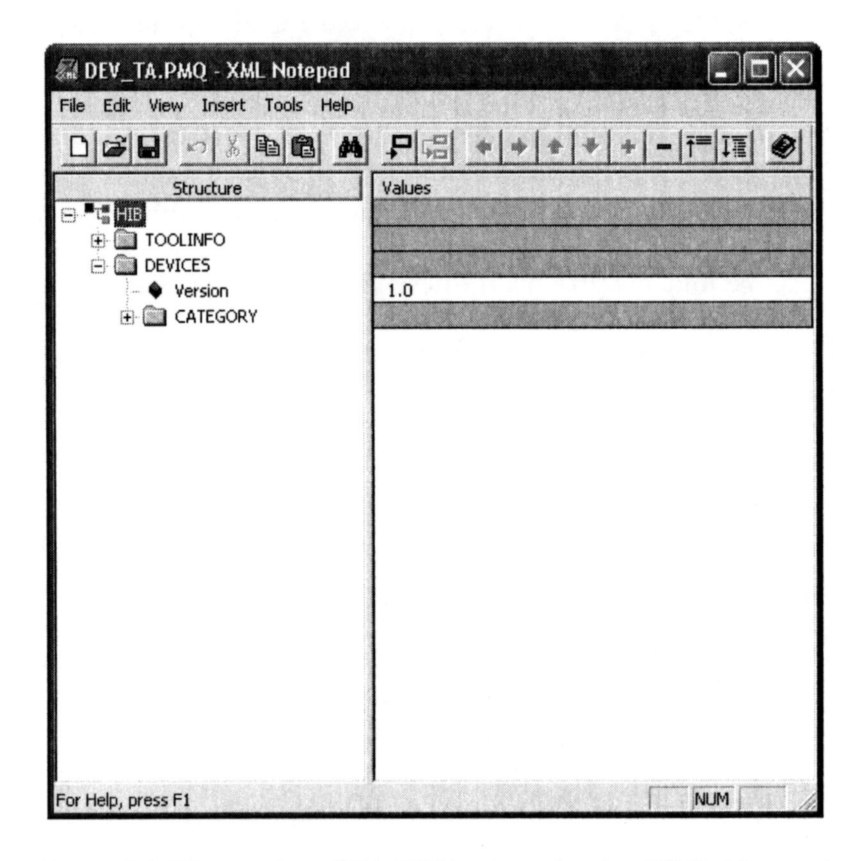

Figure 5.1 The results of TA.EXE, viewed using XML Notepad.

4. Notice that there is only a single category named **DOS**. Expand the elements and select a device element.

5. Select the **HARDWAREIDS** element under any device. You will see Plug and Play IDs that are used to search the XP Embedded database for the appropriate component.

6. Launch a second instance of XML Notepad and open **dev_tap.pmq** in it. Now you can compare the results of TA.EXE versus TAP.EXE.

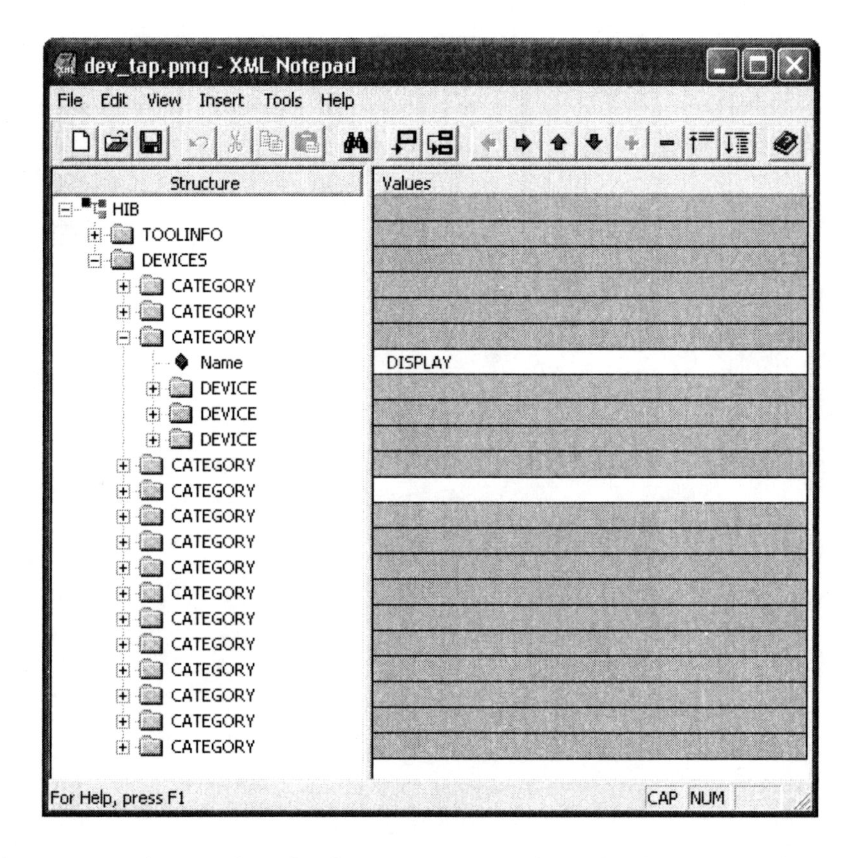

Figure 5.2 The results of using TAP.EXE, viewed using XML Notepad.

7. Notice that instead of a single CATEGORY, there are multiple categories. Expand a CATEGORY element to view the CATEGORY name.

8. Close both instances of XML Notepad when you are done examining the PMQ files.

The next step in building a Windows XP Embedded run-time image is to create a new Target Designer configuration and import a PMQ file into the configuration. This will be done in the next section.

CHAPTER 6 Target Designer

Section 6.1 Target Designer Overview

Microsoft Target Designer is the primary authoring tool for creating Windows XP Embedded run time images. The Target Designer main screen has four panes: the Component Browser, the Configuration Editor, the Details pane, and the Output pane. The Output pane also has 3 tabs: Tasks, Messages, and Debug. This section will cover all the parts of the Target Designer interface.

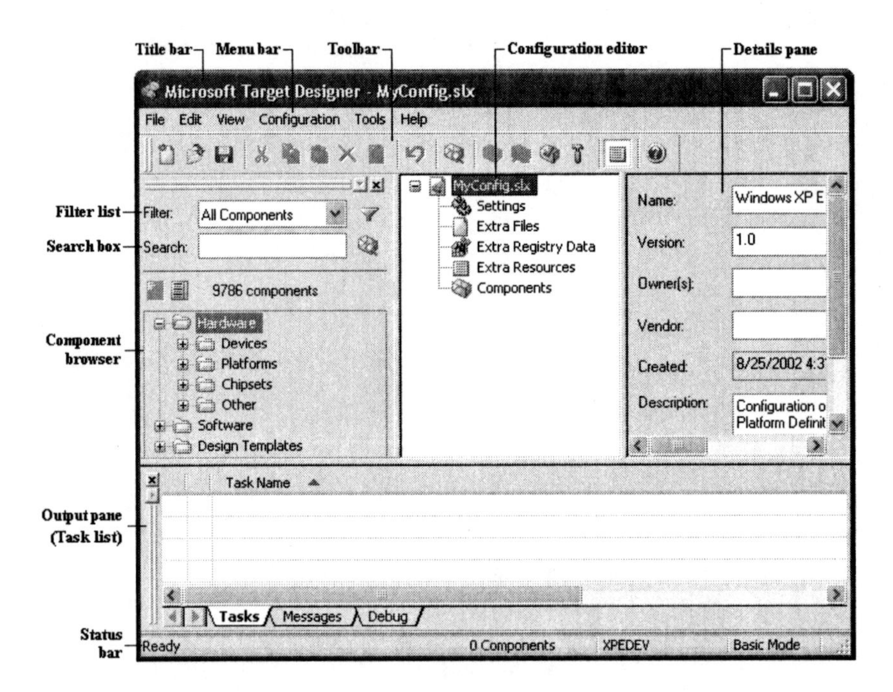

Figure 6.1 The Target Designer interface.

Section 6.1.1 Component Browser

The Component Browser lists the components in the component database. A component is the smallest individually selectable piece of functionality that can be included or excluded from a run-time image. The Filter tool, which was covered in detail under the Component Database Manager subject, can be applied to list the components which satisfy specified filter rules. There is a search utility in the Component Browser as well. Unlike the Filter, a search will find the component from within the *current* component list that matches the search criteria. It will not change the component list like the Filter tool does. Components can be viewed in the Component Browser in two ways, Tree View and List View.

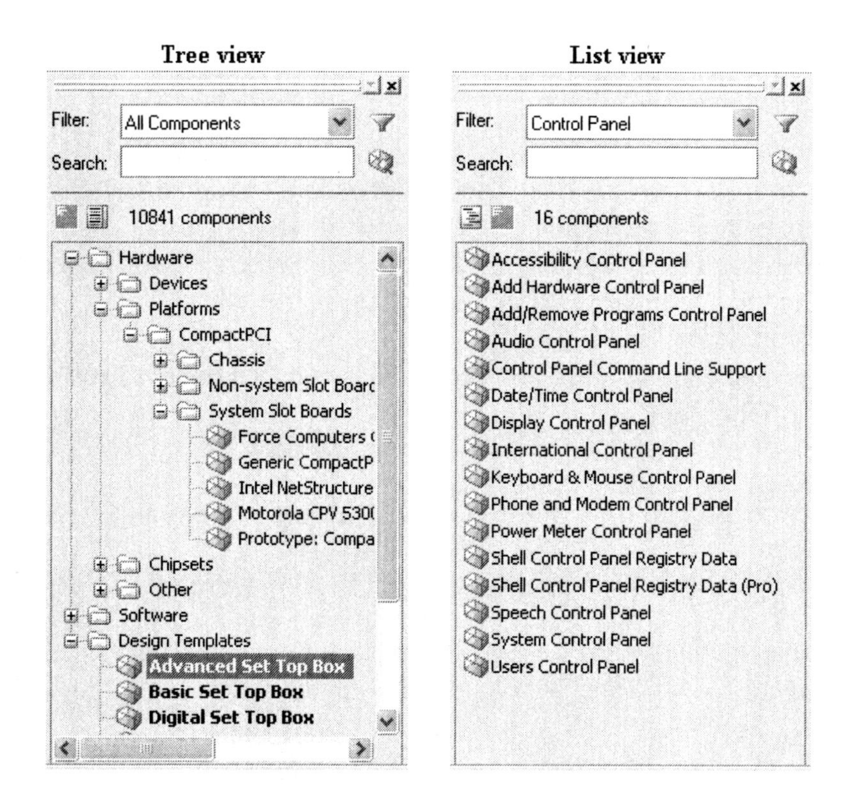

Figure 6.2 The two views available for the Component Browser.

In **Tree View** components are organized by categories. The tree view lists the components according to which group each component belongs to. Components can belong to more than one group, which can make it easier to find a component since it may logically belong to multiple groups. In **List View** components are listed alphabetically by component name. It is sometimes more convenient to use the list view when applying a filter to the component list, especially if you are not interested in which categories the components belong to.

You will notice that some component names are printed in boldface. A component with its name printed in boldface indicates that the component is a *macro* component. A macro component bundles multiple individual components together into one component. Macro components help you to quickly add a specific functionality to your configuration, or quickly build a specific type of embedded device. Macro components are listed under their appropriate category according to their functionality. There are several macro components under the Design Templates category, for example. Each one is designed for a particular embedded device scenario, such as a Set Top Box or a Retail Point of Sale Terminal to name a few. Some macro components enable you to choose the specific functionality of the macro component in the component settings. Components will be covered in further detail under the subject of Component Designer.

There are several ways to add a component from the Component Browser to a configuration:

- Double-click the component to be added.
- Right-click on the component, the select **Add** from the menu that appears.
- Drag the component from the Component Browser and drop it into the Configuration Editor.
- From the **Configuration** menu, choose **Add Component**.
- Select the component in the Component Browser, and then click the **Add** button on the toolbar (works for list view only).

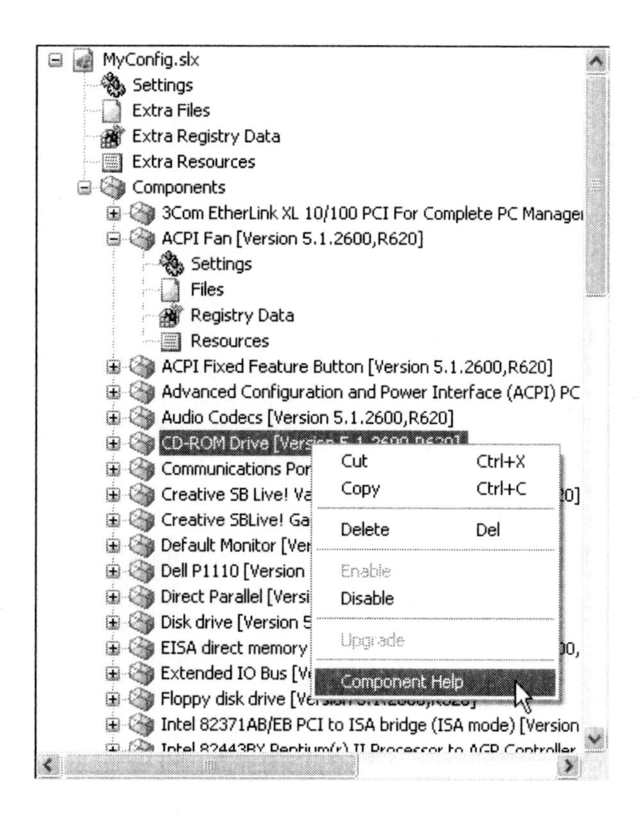

Figure 6.3 The menu in the Configuration Editor.

Section 6.1.2 Configuration Editor

The Configuration Editor shows all components that are part of a configuration. Right-clicking on a component brings up a short-cut menu where you can select a number of tasks to perform with the component, including the standard Cut, Copy, Paste and Delete. The other options available are:

- Disable - Disabling a component will leave the component in the configuration's component list, but the disabled component will not be included in the build. This can be helpful when debugging a configuration; rather than completely removing it from the configuration, it can be temporarily excluded.

- Enable - Enable a component that had been previously disabled.

- Upgrade - Upgrading a component will query the component database to check if there is a newer version of the selected component. This query can be done for all the components in the configuration by right-clicking the **Components** node at the top of the component list in the Configuration Editor, and then selecting **Upgrade**. There is also a Target Designer setting that can be set so that all components in a configuration are automatically upgraded every time the configuration is opened in Target Designer (this will be covered in more detail below).

- Component Help - If a help file exists for the component, selecting Component Help will bring up a new window which will display the contents of the component help file.

Section 6.1.3 Details Pane

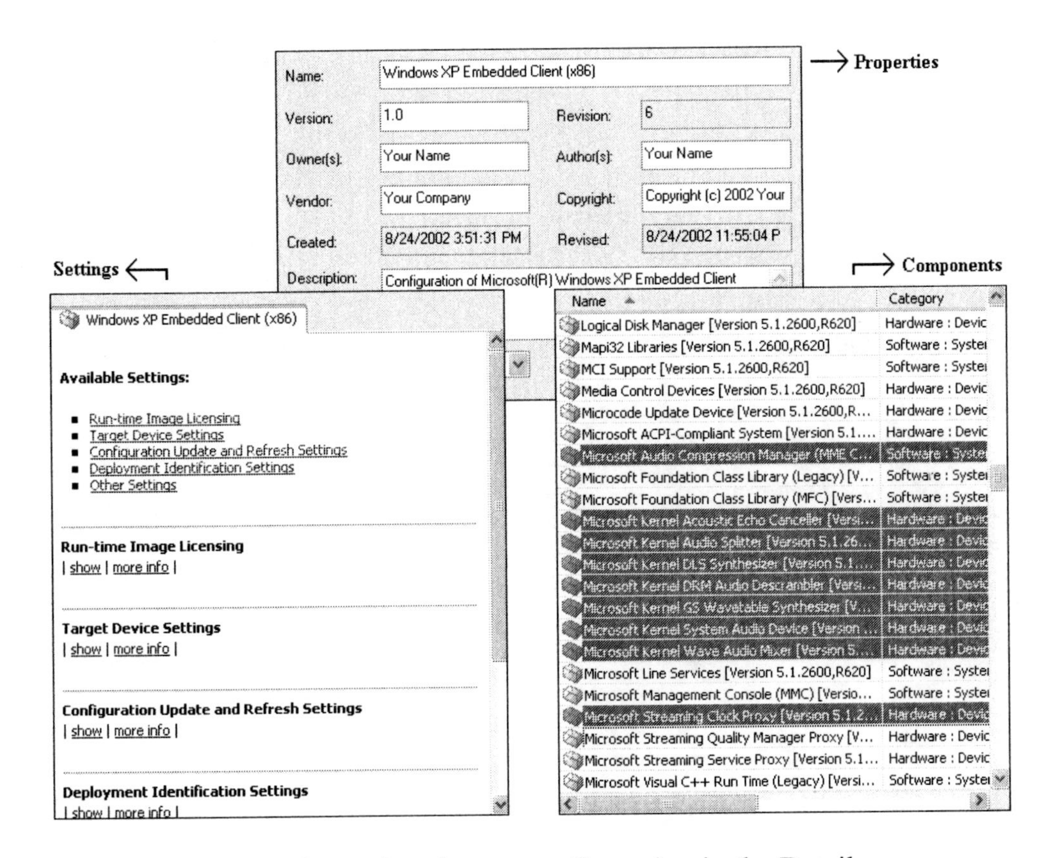

Figure 6.4 Information about a configuration in the Details pane.

The Details pane displays information about the configuration and components, including Extra Files, Extra Registry Data, and Extra Resources for the configuration. In order to view all of the available information that can be displayed in the Details pane, the **Resources** option needs to be selected from the **View** menu. Selecting the root (topmost) node in the configuration editor will display the configuration's properties. The configuration's settings will be displayed in the Details pane by selecting the **Settings** node under the configuration's root node, and the Details pane will display all of the components in the configuration by selecting the **Components** node in the Configuration Editor. The Configuration Editor only allows you to select one component at a time. If you are going to remove a number of components from the configuration, multiple components can be selected in the Details pane by holding down the CTRL button on the keyboard while selecting components in the Details pane.

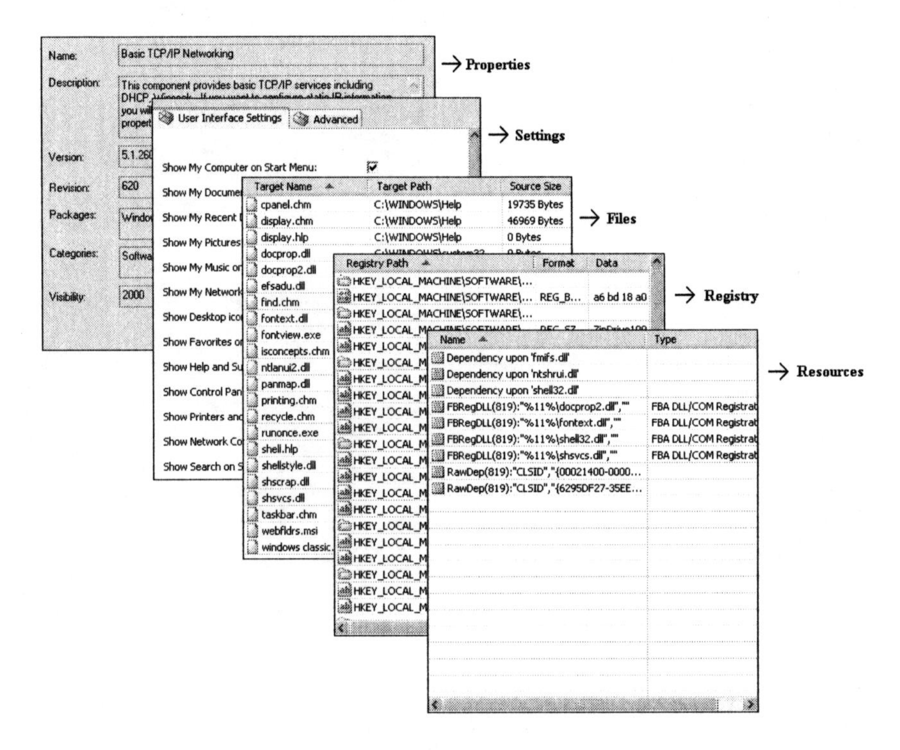

Figure 6.5 Details pane views for a component.

Additional information about a component can be viewed by expanding the component node in the Configuration Editor and selecting one of the items:

- Settings - If the component is configurable, the settings can be modified by selecting the **Settings** resource under the component node. Components that do not have settings that are specific to the component will have **General Properties** that are typical for all components.

- Files - All the files included with a component are displayed in the Details pane by selecting the **Files** resource. The list displays the name of the file when it is copied to the target system, the location where the file will be copied to on the target system, and the size of the file.

- Registry Data- The component's registry keys are displayed in the Details pane by selecting the component's **Registry Data** resource.

- Resources - Component resources, which will be covered in further detail under the subject of Component Designer, can be one of the following:

  - Large registry data
  - Component branch
  - Plug and Play device identifier
  - Service data
  - First Boot Agent
  - Dynamic Link Library (DLL)
  - Component Object Model (COM) registration

Section 6.1.4 Output Pane

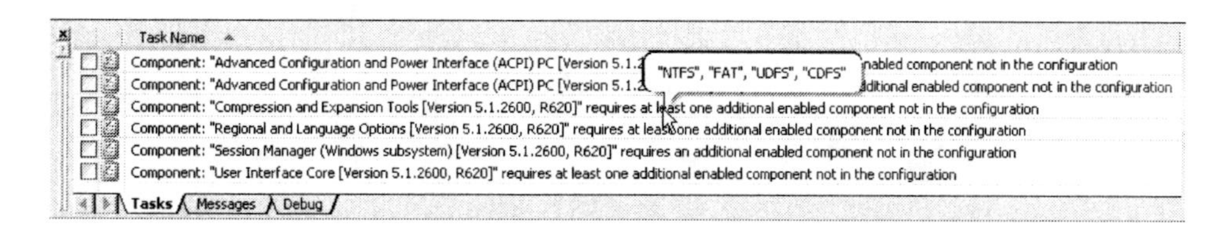

Figure 6.6 The Output pane displays the task list.

The Output pane has three tabs:

- Tasks - The tasks tab displays a list of tasks that need to be performed. Typically, tasks are added to this list when there are dependency issues following a dependency check. Double-clicking a task in the list brings up a dialog box that lists the required or conflicting components, as well as instructions on how to resolve the issue. You can also add your own tasks to the task list.

- Messages - The messages tab provides information about the function that is being executed. For example, while importing a PMQ file, performing a dependency check, or building a run-time image, the process will produce messages about what is going on and display them in the messages tab. Every function that writes information to the messages tab provides a means for specifying a log file to write to for later viewing.

- Debug - The debug tab displays messages about actions that have taken place in Target Designer, such as opening a configuration, adding or removing a component, performing a dependency check, or executing a build.

Section 6.2 Target Designer Options

Now that the basics of the interface have been covered, there are a few key details that require some description. From the **Tools** menu, selecting **Options...** will bring up an interface where you can configure some settings for Target Designer. You will see four available tabs: Mode, Build, Dependency Check and Advanced.

Section 6.2.1 Mode

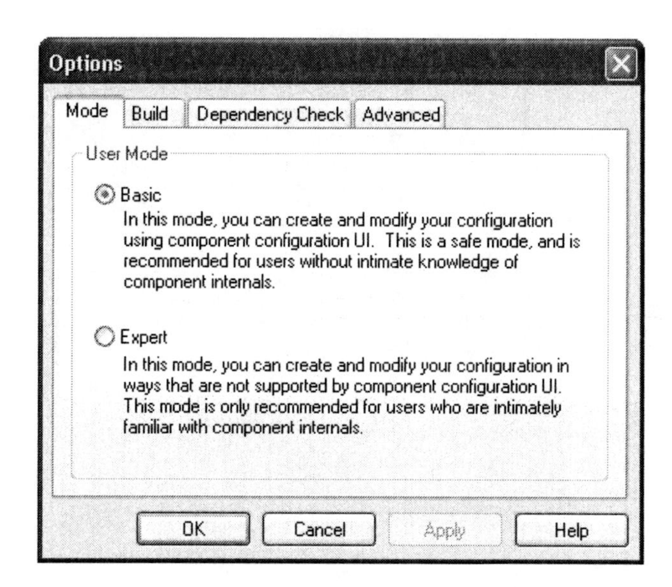

Figure 6.7 The Mode tab of the Options feature.

The Mode tab enables you to set the default user mode to either Basic or Expert. Basic mode protects the integrity of a configuration by requiring the use of the user interface to modify component or configuration settings. Expert mode enables you to create and modify your configuration in ways that are not typically supported by the configuration user interface, which could jeopardize the integrity of the configuration.

Section 6.2.2 Build

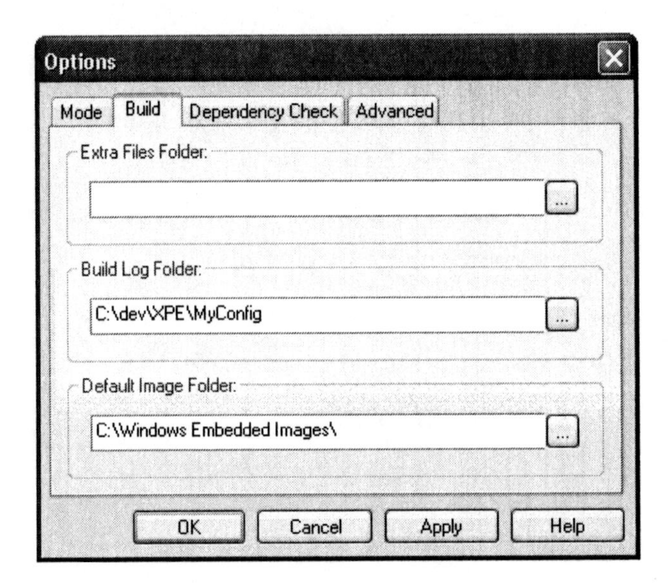

Figure 6.8 The Build tab of the Options feature.

The Build tab enables you to set default folder locations for build log files and for the image folder. These folders can be changed in the Build dialog that comes up when you select **Build Target Image...** from the **Configuration** menu, but the settings will default to the folder paths specified in the Options feature.

When developing and deploying using the same machine in a dual-boot scenario, as is being done with the exercises in this book, the default image folder can be set to build the run-time image directly to the partition where the image is to be deployed. This will save the step of copying the run-time image folders and files from the folder C\:Windows Embedded Images\ to the D:\ (or whatever secondary partition is used).

Section 6.2.3 Dependency Check

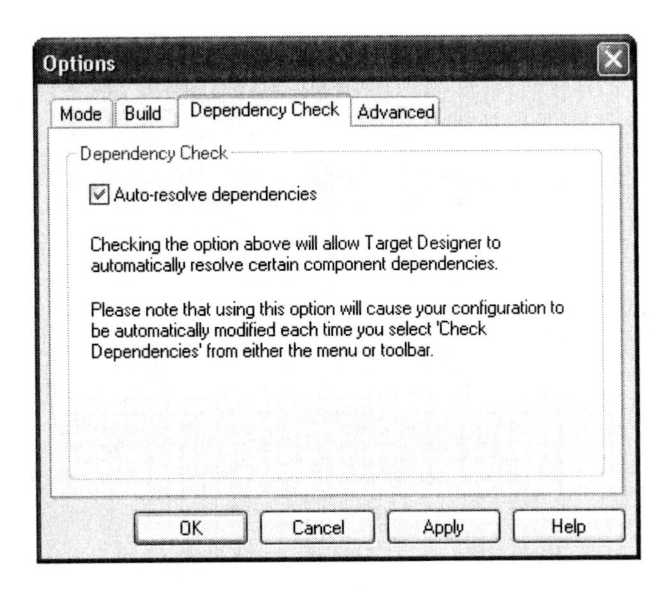

Figure 6.9 The Dependency Check tab of the Options feature.

The Dependency Check tab has only one setting, which enables the Auto-resolve dependencies feature. Enabling this feature will allow the dependency checker to automatically resolve all the dependency errors that it is capable of resolving. For example, if a component that you added to your configuration requires a specific component that has not been previously added to your configuration, Target Designer will automatically add the required component for you when the dependency checker comes across the error. Only the dependency errors that require you to choose a component from a selection will appear in the task list. With the auto-resolve dependencies feature disabled, components will not be automatically added or removed from your configuration and all dependency errors will appear in the task list. This list can be rather large, but it is a method that can be used to try to control exactly which components go into your configuration. It might be useful to disable the auto-resolve dependencies feature if you are concerned about keeping the size of your image down, but you will need to resolve any conflicts manually.

Section 6.2.4 Advanced

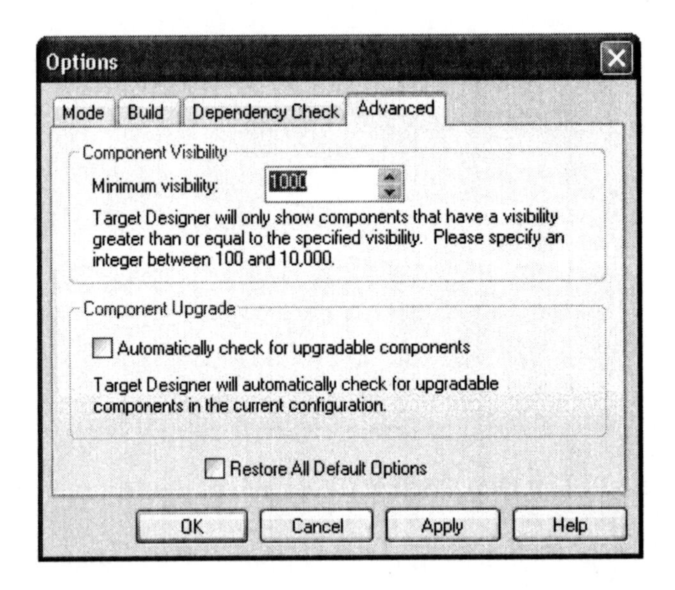

Figure 6.10 The Advanced tab of the Options feature.

Every component in the database has a visibility level setting. You can use the Component Visibility setting in the Advanced tab of the Options feature to set a minimum visibility level, which keeps smaller or less significant components from cluttering up the Component Browser list. The component list in the Component Browser will display only the components which have a visibility level greater than or equal to the specified minimum visibility setting. It acts like a filter, but only has this one rule.

An earlier section described how to manually perform a component upgrade in the Configuration Editor. There is also an Options feature that will tell Target Designer to automatically check your configuration for any components that can be upgraded. Target Designer will automatically query the database and replace each component that has a newer version of the component in the database.

In the next exercises, you will prepare the deployment partition, set up the system for dual booting, create a new configuration, import the results from TAP.EXE into the configuration, perform dependency checks, build a run-time image from the configuration, and then deploy and boot the run-time image. The section that follows the exercise provides some tips for troubleshooting common problems.

Section 6.3 EXERCISE 6

Prepare the media and system for dual booting

1. Open **My Computer** from the **Start**.

2. Right-click on the D: drive (or your desired partition) and select **Format**. Warning! This will overwrite any and all data on the partition. Be certain that this is the correct partition or drive before proceeding.

3. On the Format dialog box, select **FAT** from the **File System** pull-down menu, click the **Quick Format** checkbox, then click the **Start** button.

4. Click the **OK** button on the warning dialog box that appears.

5. Click the **OK** button when the "Format complete" message dialog appears, then click the **Close** button on the Format dialog.

6. In the root directory of the C: drive, open the file **Boot.ini** using a text editor, such as Notepad. Boot.ini is a hidden system file. If you cannot see the file in the root directory, you may have to adjust the settings on the **View** tab of the file explorer's **Folder Options**, which can be opened from the **Tools** menu in the **My Computer** file explorer, so that hidden files will be shown.

7. Append the following line to the Boot.ini file:

   multi(0)disk(0)rdisk(0)partition(2)\WINDOWS="Microsoft Windows XP Embedded" /fastdetect

Note: There are a couple other changes that you can make to the Boot.ini file for convenience purposes. The "default=" setting can be changed so that the default operating system selection will be "Microsoft Windows XP Embedded" instead of "Microsoft Windows XP Professional" (or 2000) when the system boots up. Just change the number on the right side of the word "partition" from 1 to 2. Also, you can reduce the "timeout=" setting, which is the number of seconds that the system will wait for you to make a selection before continuing with the default selection (5 to 10 seconds is a reasonable amount of time). As the First Boot Agent (FBA) is running during the very first boot of your XP Embedded run-time image, it will reboot the system a few times as it is performing initialization. The reason behind these particular changes to Boot.ini is so that the system will not require any user interaction when you are booting the Windows XP Embedded operating system for the very first time. You can just let the FBA do its job and reboot the system as many times as needed, and you won't have to select "Microsoft Windows XP Embedded" every time the FBA does a reboot.

8. Save and close the Boot.ini file. Both partitions are now available for booting.

Section 6.4 EXERCISE 7

Create a new Target Designer configuration and import the TAP.exe output file

1. Launch Target Designer. From the **Start** menu, click **All Programs**, select **Windows Embedded Studio**, and then click **Target Designer.**

2. From the **File** menu, select **New** and name the configuration **TAPBASE,** then click the **OK** button.

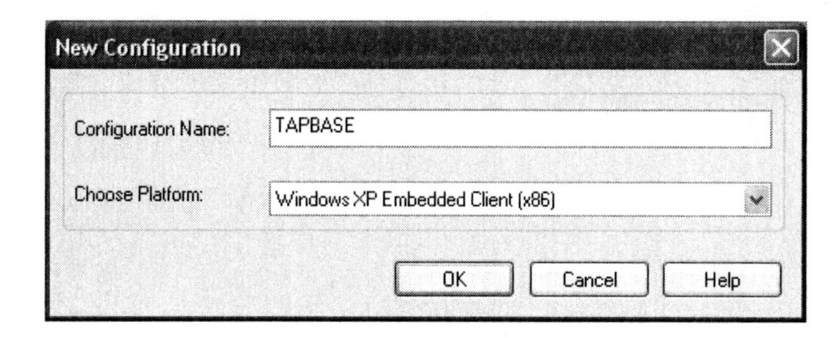

Figure 6.11 The New Configuration dialog box.

3. In the Configuration Editor, expand the configuration root, TAPBASE.slx, and click on **Settings**. If **Settings** is the only one displayed under the configuration root node and you wish to view the other resources in the configuration editor, select **Resources** from the **View** menu.

4. In the Details Pane under **Available Settings**, click the **Target Device Settings** link, and then click on the **show** link. Since the image is to be deployed to the hard drive's second partition (the D: drive), the settings should be set as in the figure below.

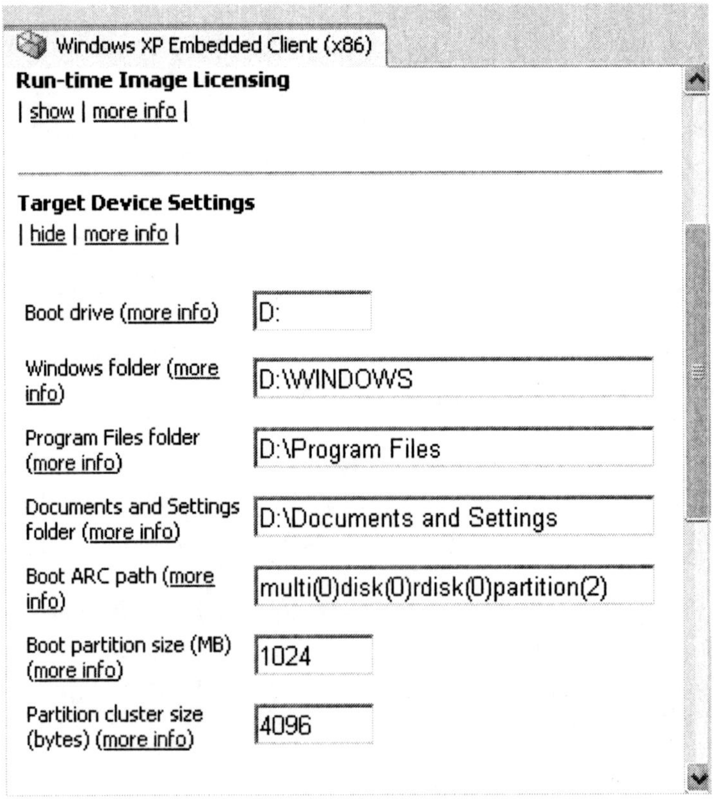

Windows XP Embedded Client (x86)

Run-time Image Licensing

| show | more info |

Target Device Settings

| hide | more info |

Boot drive (more info) D:

Windows folder (more info) D:\WINDOWS

Program Files folder (more info) D:\Program Files

Documents and Settings folder (more info) D:\Documents and Settings

Boot ARC path (more info) multi(0)disk(0)rdisk(0)partition(2)

Boot partition size (MB) (more info) 1024

Partition cluster size (bytes) (more info) 4096

Figure 6.12 The configuration's Target Device Settings.

*Note: Above the **Target Device Settings** in the details pane displaying the configuration settings you will notice a setting labeled **Run-time Image Licensing**. Clicking the **show** link will enable you to fill in the **Product ID key** property with the product ID key for licensing the run-time image. If this property is left blank, the build will be considered a test build and expire between 90 and 180 days. The product ID key is obtained by purchasing a Windows XP operating system license from an authorized distributor. It is not required to complete the exercises in this book.*

5. From the **File** menu, select **Import**, browse to the folder named **C:\XPE dev\TA_DATA**, and then select the file **dev_tap.pmq.** This assumes that the Target Analyzer Exercise 5 has been completed. If not, return to Exercise 5 in Chapter 5 and follow the instructions.

6. On the **Import File** dialog, copy the path from the **File** text box to the **Log File** text box. Append the path with the log file name **tap import.log**.

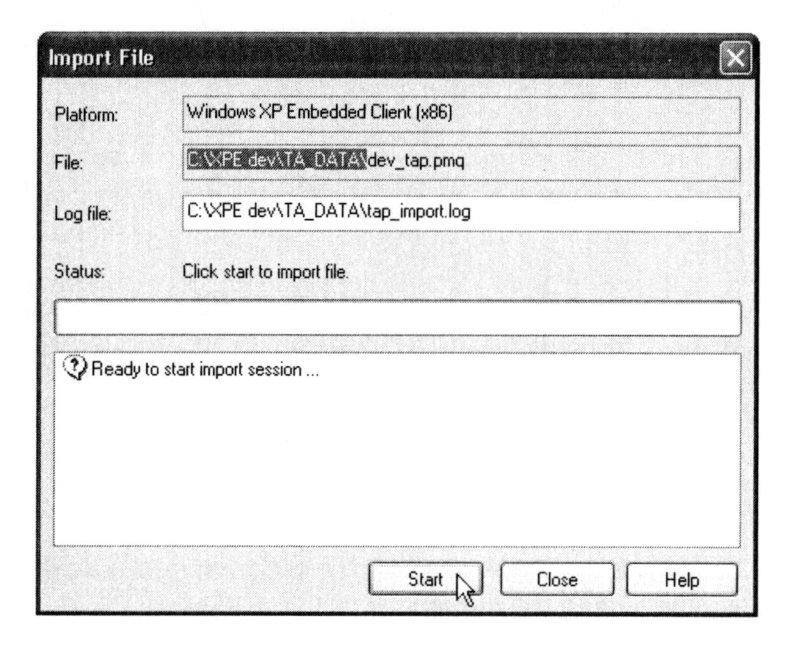

Figure 6.13 The Import File dialog box for importing the results of Target Analyzer.

7. Click the **Start** button. The import process may take several minutes.

8. Once the PMQ import is complete, click the **Close** button to close the **Import File** dialog.

9. From the **File** menu, select **Save As**, and then browse to the folder C:\ **XPE dev\TA_DATA**. Make sure that the name of the file is **TAPBASE.slx**, then click the **Save** button.

Note: It is a good practice to save the configuration in stages so that you can revert the configuration to a previously saved state. You should save a separate copy of the configuration immediately following the PMQ file import. That way, you won't have to go through the lengthy PMQ file import process again when you go to create a new configuration for the same hardware. Skip the steps labeled (Optional) if you do not wish to save the configuration while it is in the post-import state.

10. (Optional) From the **File** menu, select **Save As**. Right-click on the file **TAPBASE.slx** and select **Copy**. On the keyboard, press the Ctrl key and the 'v' key at the same time.

11. (Optional) Right-click on the file **Copy of TAPBASE.slx** and select **Rename**. Rename the copied file **TAPPostImport.slx**, then click the **Cancel** button.

Note: For future reference, this is a good point to remove unwanted components from your configuration if you are looking to reduce the size of your image. With the auto-resolve feature enabled, Target Designer will add a lot more components during the first dependency check, which will make more work for you later. For this exercise, we will leave all the components where they are.

Perform a dependency check and resolve all dependency errors

1. To perform a dependency check, select **Check Dependencies** from the **Configuration** menu. The auto-resolve feature should be enabled. Close the **Dependency Check** dialog after the dependency check is complete.

Note: Before performing a dependency check with auto-resolve enabled, you might want to first perform a dependency check with auto-resolve disabled, just so you can see the difference it makes.

2. With auto-resolve enabled, there will still be some dependency errors that need to be manually resolved. Double click a task in the **Task List** to manually resolve a dependency error. After all dependency errors in the **Task List** have been resolved, run another dependency check. The procedure of running a dependency check and resolving dependency errors will need to be repeated until no dependency errors are present. Below are some typical dependency errors that you may have to resolve.

Note: A component may have the same system requirement and dependency error resolution as another component, so you might see duplicate resolutions. For example, in this configuration there are two components that require file system support. One way to handle duplicate dependency resolutions is by repeating the action, which will not have any effect on the configuration; it will only indicate to Target Designer that the dependency error has been resolved. Another way is to check the checkbox next to the component task in the task list that has the duplicate dependency error resolution. You can also choose to completely ignore the dependency error task, but it may show up again after another dependency check if the appropriate action has not been performed. A warning dialog will appear if you attempt to perform a build without resolving dependency errors.

Task	System Requirement	Resolution
Component: "Advance Configuration and Power Interface (ACPI) PC [...]"	Boot loader.	Add "NT Loader" component.
Component: "Advance Configuration and Power Interface (ACPI) PC [...]"	File system.	Add both "FAT" and "NTFS" components.
Component: "Compression and Expansion Tools[...]"	File system (duplicate).	Add both "FAT" and "NTFS" components.
Component: "Regional and Language Options [...]"	Language support.	Add the "English Language Support" component.
Component: "Session Manager (Windows subsystem) [...]"configuration.	Login process.	Add the "Windows Logon (Standard)" component.
Component: "User Interface Core [...]"	Required utilities.	Add the "FAT Format" and "NTFS Format" components.
Component: "Windows Logon (Standard) [...]"	Shell.	Add the "Explorer shell" component.

Table 6.1 Typical Dependency Errors

3. Add the **Task Manager** component. It can be found in the component browser under the category **Software : System : User Interface : Shells : Windows Shell**.

Build and deploy the run-time image

1. After completing a dependency check without errors, the next step is to build the image. From the **Configuration** menu, select **Build Target Image…**.

2. You might have already set the default folder locations on the **Build** tab in Target Designer's **Options** window. If so, the folders you specified will show up on the **Build** window, otherwise you can change the paths so that they are the same as in the figure below. Click the **Build** button when the folders' locations are set.

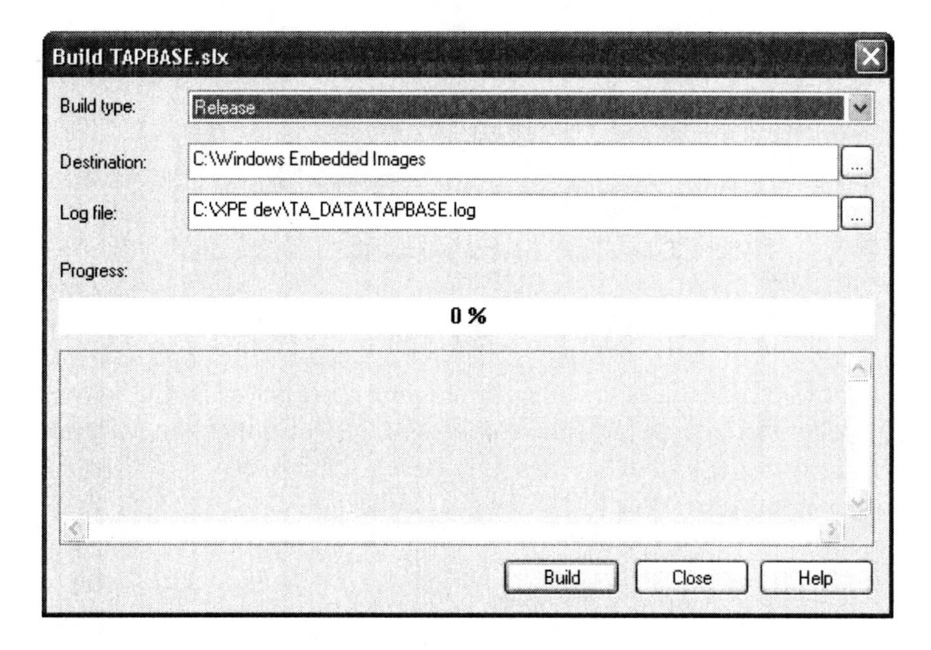

Figure 6.14 Target Designer's Build window.

3. Sometimes a warning dialog will appear after clicking the **Build** button. The only time that this warning dialog will not show up is if you execute the build command immediately following your final dependency check, with-

out doing anything else between the steps. If, for example, you performed your final dependency check with no errors, then you saved your configuration before executing the build command, the warning dialog will prompt you to perform a dependency check. The only time that you really have to perform a dependency check is if components are added or removed from a configuration. If you are positive that no components have been added or removed from your configuration, you do not have to perform an additional dependency check just because the pop-up dialog highly recommends it. Click the **No** button.

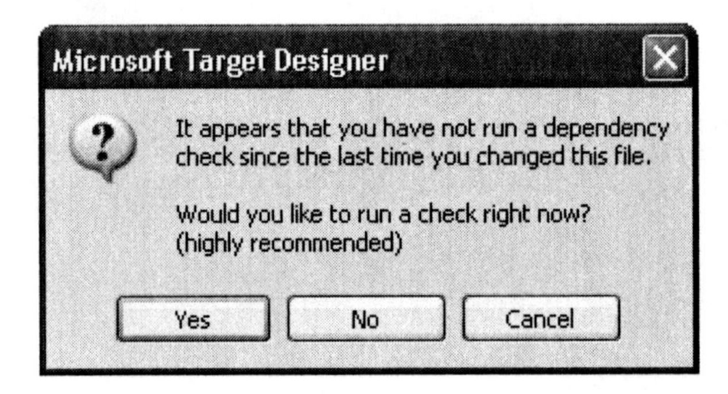

Figure 6.15 The pre-build dependency check warning dialog.

4. Another warning dialog that will appear when clicking the **Build** button will ask if you would like to clear the contents of the run-time image destination folder. This dialog will always appear, even if the destination folder is already empty. Select **Yes**.

Figure 6.16 The pre-build delete files warning dialog.

5. The Windows XP Embedded run-time image will now be built. Target Designer will copy the components' binaries and build the run-time image's directory tree under the destination folder that was specified in the build window, which is **C:\Windows Embedded Images**. The messages that are printed under the progress bar will be written to the log file specified. When the build is complete, there should be no errors and one warning. The warning states that the build is a test build which will expire between 90 and 180 days, because a product ID was not entered to license the image. Close the build window after the build has successfully completed.

6. Save the configuration and close Target Designer.

7. Open **My Computer** and browse to C:\Windows Embedded Images. Copy all the folders and files, which is essentially the run-time image, from within **C:\Windows Embedded Images** to the **D:** drive but do *not* copy the **Windows Embedded Images** folder itself. Reboot the system and select the Windows XP Embedded OS if it is not selected by default.

8. The Windows XP Embedded image is not functional until the First Boot Agent successfully executes. Execution of the FBA will take several minutes. When the FBA successfully completes, your XP Embedded desktop will appear.

Section 6.5 Troubleshooting Tips

There are a few common errors that may occur when attempting to boot the Windows XP Embedded operating system for the first time. The problem usually ends up being a setting that is not configured properly. The target device settings and boot.ini settings specified in the exercises may not work for the system that you are using.

One of the most common errors occurs after the Windows XP Embedded option is selected from the boot menu, causing the screen to go black and print an error messaging stating that the boot ARC path is incorrect or that the operating system could not be found; the First Boot Agent does not even start. The first step to begin troubleshooting this problem is to boot to XP Professional and open the disk manager: right-click on **My Computer**, select **Manage**, and then click on **Disk Management**. Make sure that the partition is formatted as FAT or FAT32. The disk manager can also be used to verify that the proper partition number of the boot ARC path is specified in the Target Device Settings and in boot.ini. Independent of the drive letter that is assigned by the OS, the partition number in the boot ARC path is typically determined by the order in which the partitions exist on the disk. The figure below from the disk manager shows that the C: drive is partition 1, the D: drive is partition 2, and the F: drive is partition 3.

Figure 6.17 The partition number is typically determined by the order that the partitions exist on the disk.

Another common error is that the First Boot Agent starts but repeatedly reboots the system. If this occurs, it is probably because the drive letters assigned in the configuration's **Target Device Settings** in Target Designer are incorrect. In order to determine the correct drive letter, the FBA log file, **FBALOG.txt**, can be viewed.

It is located on the partition containing XP Embedded image, in the folder **\WINDOWS\fba**.

If the FBA generates an exception error and you get a virtual memory error during FBA, that means that your run-time image has loaded more services and registered more binaries than the system has physical RAM for. You can either reduce the number of features by removing components from the configuration (not recommended for absolute beginners), add pagefile support, or add more RAM. To add pagefile support, you need to modify the Target Designer settings of whichever computer component is included in the configuration, such as the **Standard PC** component or the **Advanced Configuration and Power Interface PC** component.

The most challenging common error causes the "blue screen of death" to appear with an error code such as "0x0000007B". The most common reason for this is because the run-time image does not include all of the components required in order to have a working operating system. TAP.exe typically finds all of the required components. If you used the results from TA.exe to create your run-time image, chances are that not all of the required components were detected. The dependency check does not always detect when a component that is required to have a working image is missing. Make sure that the Target Designer configuration includes the following required types of devices:

- IDE Controllers
- PCI/ISA Bridges or Controllers
- Memory Access Controllers
- Keyboard/Mouse Components
- Display Adapter

Later, in the Embedded Enabling Features chapter, there will be an exercise that builds a new configuration based on the results from TA.exe, in an attempt to reduce the size of the image footprint.

Section 6.6 The Windows XP Embedded Desktop

Figure 6.18 The TAPBASE XP Embedded run-time image desktop.

The desktop of the Windows XP Embedded image that you just built may appear to not have as much functionality as you might have expected: there are only two items on the start menu, you can't change the desktop wallpaper, the Control Panel is not present, etc. Certain components and settings need to be built into the image in order to utilize some of the familiar Windows desktop capabilities. For example, if you want to be able to change the time, you will need to add the Date/Time Control Panel component. If you only add the Control Panel component, you will be able to launch the Control Panel, but you will not be able to use any of the Control Panel applets until you build the particular Control Panel applet components into your image. Remember that one of the main features of building an XP Embedded image for your platform is so that you can take advantage of this type of control.

The category **Software : System : User Interface : Shells : Windows Shell** in the component browser contains several of the components that will make your XP Embedded run-image more desktop friendly. The name and description of each component basically explains the function of the component. Other "desktop" components can be found under different categories by using the Filter Tool. The remaining exercises in this book will not require any of these components to be built into the image. If you wish to build a "desktop friendly" image, you should create a new, separate configuration for adding the extra components. You can simply open TAPBASE.slx in Target Designer, immediately save it as TAPDesktop.slx, add the components, perform the dependency checks, then build and deploy the image. Use the steps in the previous exercise as a guide.

Some of the components you wish to add will not need to be added because they have already been added to your TAPBASE configuration, such as the Windows Logon component and the User Interface Core component (by the way, the User Interface Core component has settings that will enable you to add items to the Start menu and modify a few other desktop properties). Some components will be added by a dependency check. For example, if you add the Screen Savers component, a dependency check (with auto-resolve enabled) will add the component Shell Screen Saver Registry Data. The dependency checker will add every component that goes along with the featured component you wish to add. Any duplicate components you add to the configuration will appear grayed-out in the Configuration Editor (unless the component allows duplicates); delete them because they are not going to get built into the image anyway. Just keep in mind that even if you were to add every single desktop component to your image that XP Embedded has to offer, you still will not be able to make an XP Embedded image that will function exactly like a desktop version of XP. Each version has differences that make it appropriate for its purpose.

CHAPTER 7 Component Designer

To include an application or a driver in a run-time image, you must first define the application or driver as a component using Component Designer. In addition to defining components, Component Designer enables you to define Repositories, Packages, Dependencies, and Repository Sets. The resulting output of Component Designer is called a System Level Definition, or SLD, file. The SLD file is actually an XML text file. One or more objects can be defined in an SLD file.

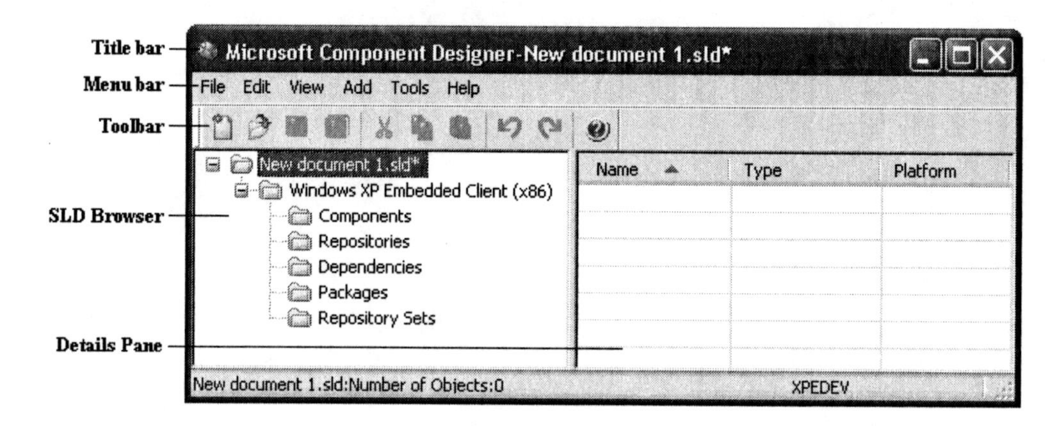

Figure 7.1 The Component Designer interface.

There are two window panes in the Component Designer interface: the SLD Browser and the Details Pane. The **SLD Browser** displays a tree view of the objects defined by the SLD file. Objects are listed under their respective object-type folders. Any number of objects can be created in an SLD file. An object is created by clicking on the object-type folder within the SLD Browser and selecting an action from the **Add** menu. The **Add** menu can also be brought up in the form of a pop-up menu by right-clicking the object-type folder, or by selecting the object-type folder in the SLD browser and right-clicking anywhere in the Details pane. More than one SLD file can be opened and examined in the same instance of Component Designer. The **Details Pane** displays information according to what is selected in the SLD Browser. If the root SLD folder is selected in the SLD browser, all objects that are defined by that SLD file are listed, and if an object-type folder is selected in the SLD browser, all objects of that type are listed. When an object is selected in the SLD browser, the object's properties will be displayed in the details pane. If a resource of an object, for example a component's files, are selected in the SLD browser, the resources of the selected type that are included in the component (the files in this example) will be displayed in the Details pane.

The next section will cover properties that every object type has. The remainder of the chapter will cover each of the different types of objects that can be included in the SLD file, as well as their resources.

Section 7.1 Typical Object Properties

Every object created in Component Designer has its own properties associated with it. The object's properties are displayed in the details pane when the object is selected in the SLD Browser. There are properties that are typical for, but not common to, every object type, and then there are properties that are specific to the object type. The figure shows the properties that are typical of each object.

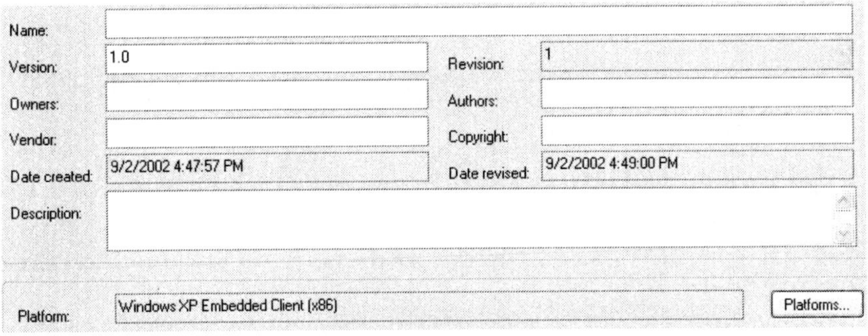

Figure 7.2 Typical properties for all object types.

When creating custom objects, the name of the object should reflect the object's purpose, and a good description of the object should be included as well. It is very helpful in conveying what the object is used for, especially when the object is a component. If a name is not specified, Component Designer will assign a GUID as the object name, and this is how it will appear when listed in any of the other tools (Component Database Manager, Target Designer, Filter tool, etc.) after the SLD file has been imported into the database.

You can see that some of the typical properties appear grayed-out and cannot be manually changed: **Revision**, **Date created**, and **Date revised**. These properties are automatically maintained by Component Designer. Every time that the SLD file is saved after any changes are made to the object, the **Revision** number is incrementally increased and the **Date revised** is updated. The version number defaults to 1.0, but that can be changed by the user.

The **Platform** property, which also appears grayed-out, can be changed by clicking the **Platforms** button. The Platform property is grouped with the object-specific properties in the details pane, even though this property must be specified for every object. Each Component Designer object, as well as every Target Designer configuration, is created for a specific platform. When a Target Designer configuration is created, only the components that were created for the same platform as the Target Designer configuration will appear in the component browser. An object's **Platform** property identifies the platform for which the object is being created. Currently, only the x86 platform is supported by Windows XP Embedded.

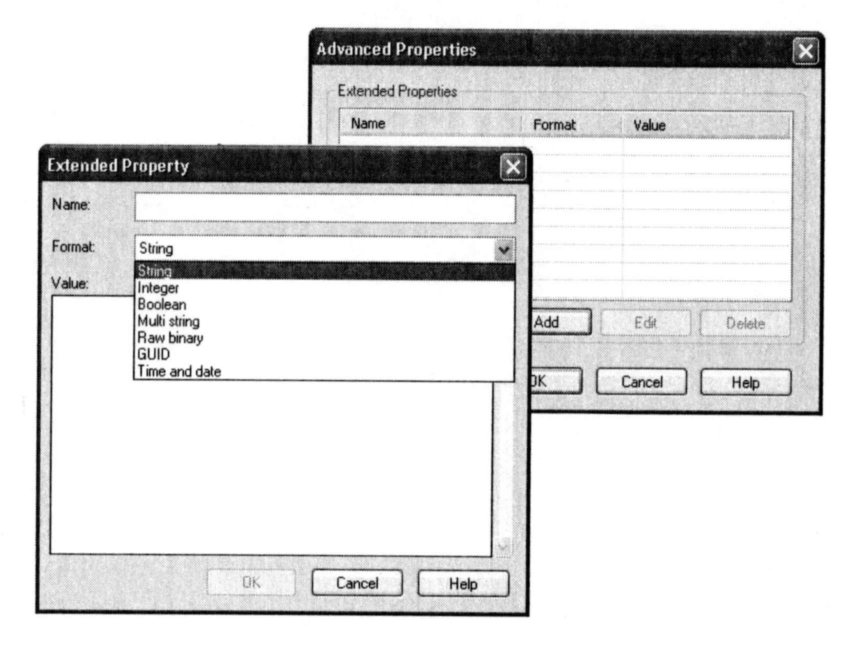

Figure 7.3 Adding an Extended Property to an object's Advance Properties.

Towards the bottom right hand corner of an object's properties page in the details pane is the **Advanced** button. Clicking the **Advanced** button in the properties window of an object, resource, or configuration will bring up the **Advanced Properties** dialog box. Extended Properties can be manually added, edited, or deleted in this dialog. Extended properties are typically used to store optional parameters or configuration information for an object, or to conditionally enable a feature. Extended properties are also used by platforms and by DHTML. An extended property has a name, data format, and data value. The data type is determined by the data format. Extended properties are added manually for most object and resource types.

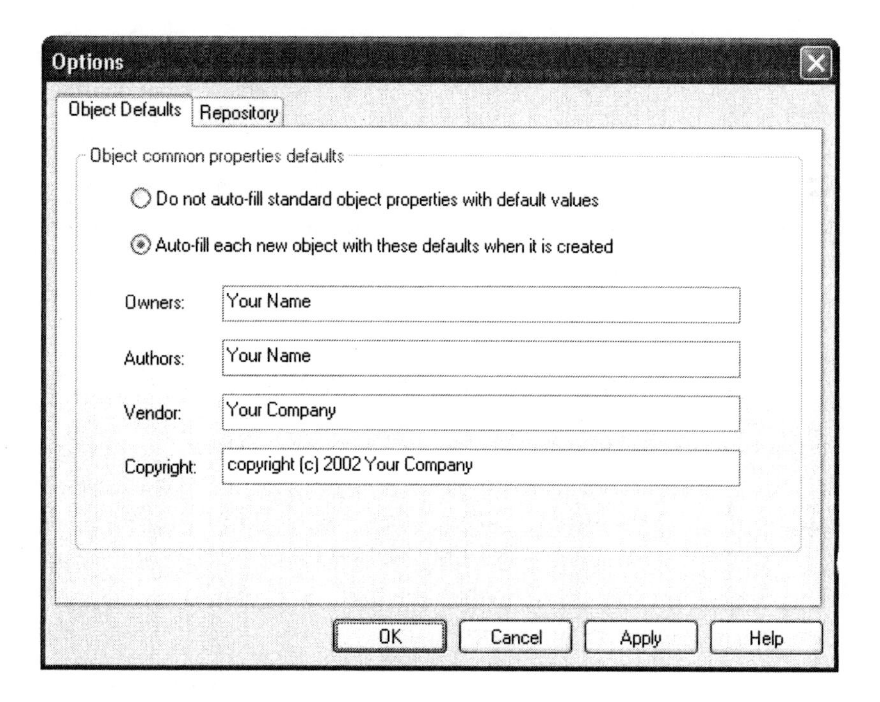

Figure 7.4 The Auto-fill option of Component Designer.

The remaining properties describe the ownership of the object: **Owners**, **Authors**, **Vendor**, and **Copyright**. Component Designer can be set up so that these particular properties are automatically filled with the same information for every object created in Component Designer. From the **Tools** pull-down menu, select **Options**. On the **Object Defaults** tab, click on **Auto-fill each new object with these defaults when it is created**, then fill in the fields with the values you wish to have as defaults.

Each object type has additional properties that are specific to the object type. The Dependency, Package, and Repository Set object types have only properties. The Component and Repository object types, in addition, have resources that can be added to the object. A file resource is an example of one of the resource types that can be included in a Component object. Each object type and its resources will be covered in the sections that follow.

Section 7.2 Repositories

Repositories are where the component database keeps the files used to build the run-time image. The files that do not use or reference repositories are those which are created dynamically during the build process, such as registry hive files. A repository is a database item which has a folder in the file system associated with it. By default, the folder of the repository object exists on the machine that contains the component database, under the directory \Windows Embedded Data\Repositories\, and it contains the actual files that are referenced by a component. If a component is to include any files, the component must specify a repository. In order to group related files together, it is customary to create a repository for a new component or group of related components that are to include files. The relationship between components and repositories enables Target Designer to locate and copy files into the target directory during the build process.

Section 7.2.1 Creation and Use of Repositories in the Build Process

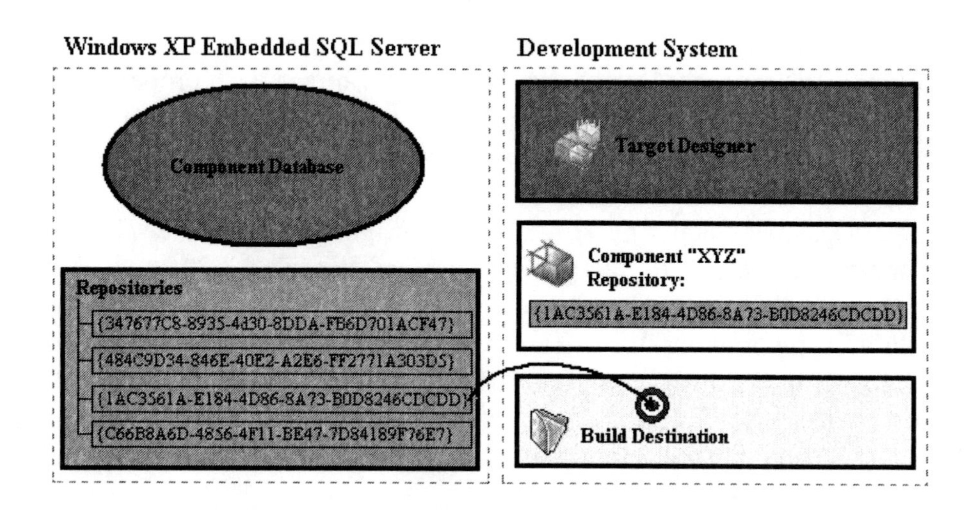

Figure 7.5 Example of how repositories work. If working with a standalone system, the SQL server and development system are the same computer.

Repository objects are created in Component Designer by right-clicking on the **Repositories** node and selecting **Add Repository**. A new repository object will show up under the **Repositories** node; you will need to give it a name and fill in the other properties appropriately in the details pane. An important property of the repository object is the Source Path. When the SLD file is imported into the database using Component Database Manager, repository objects are examined and used to create repository folders in the file system. The folders are in a central location where all who have access to the database can obtain the files. Component Database Manager copies the files from their original location, which is specified in the Source Path property, to this central location. Internally, the database references a repository by assigning a Globally Unique Identifier (GUID) as the name of the file repository folder. As Target Designer builds a run-time image, all files that are included by components are copied from the repository folders to the build destination folder.

Section 7.2.2 Repository Properties and Resources

In addition to the typical object properties, a repository has its own specific properties. When an SLD file containing a repository is imported into the component database using Component Database Manager, the **Source Path** property specifies the location of the folder which contains the file or files that are to be copied into the newly created repository. This folder should not contain any subfolders.

The Target Designer chapter indicated that a configuration could be set to build a debug or a release version of the operating system. When a repository is created, the type of operating system that the repository is to be used with can be specified in the **Build Type** property. When Target Designer builds a debug version of the operating system, files will be copied from debug repositories. If only a release repository exists while Target Designer is performing a debug build, then the files will be copied from the release repository.

A repository has one type of resource that may be added: **Group Membership**. Components can also have group memberships, which will be discussed later in the section describing components. Groups are a way of organizing items together so that operations can be performed on the group as a unit. Group memberships are not determined by the groups themselves, but rather by the objects that claim membership to the group, which is accomplished by adding a group membership resource to the object. A repository can be a member of two types of groups: Repository Sets and Packages.

Section 7.3 Repository Sets

A **Repository Set** is one of the types of groups that can be created in a Component Designer SLD. As the name implies, a repository set will have only repositories as its members. Since group memberships are not determined by the groups themselves, any type of group, including the repository set, will not have any members when it is first created. When a repository set group membership resource is added to a repository object, then the repository set specified will have that repository as a member. A component can reference a repository set, instead of just a single repository, as the source of its files. Repository sets are typically used to group repositories by build type (debug or release).

Members of a repository set can be listed using Component Database Manager. Click the **Group** tab, select a repository set from the list under **Available repository sets**, and click the **Properties** button. A repository set can be deleted by selecting a repository set and clicking the **Delete Repository Set** button.

Section 7.4 Packages

A **Package** is a type of group that can have repositories and components as its members. Using a package is a convenient way to manage multiple instances of these two object types and treat the collection as one unit. The **Component** tab of Component Database Manager can display all of the components that belong to a selected package. All members of a package (components and/or repositories) can be listed by selecting a package under **Available packages** on the **Package** tab and clicking the **Properties** button. The list displays the item name and type. A package can be deleted by clicking the **Delete** button on the **Package** tab. All components and repositories that are members of the package group will be removed from the database when a package is deleted.

Section 7.5 Components

A component is defined as "the smallest individually-selectable piece of functionality that can be included or excluded from a run-time image." Most of the work in creating an XP Embedded run-time image goes towards creating custom components that are to be included in the image. There are lots of properties and resources to configure in order to have a working component. The sections that follow will go over all of them.

Section 7.5.1 Component Properties

In addition to the typical properties mentioned previously, there are more specific properties that help define a component. Some of these properties have some form of a browse button to the right of them.

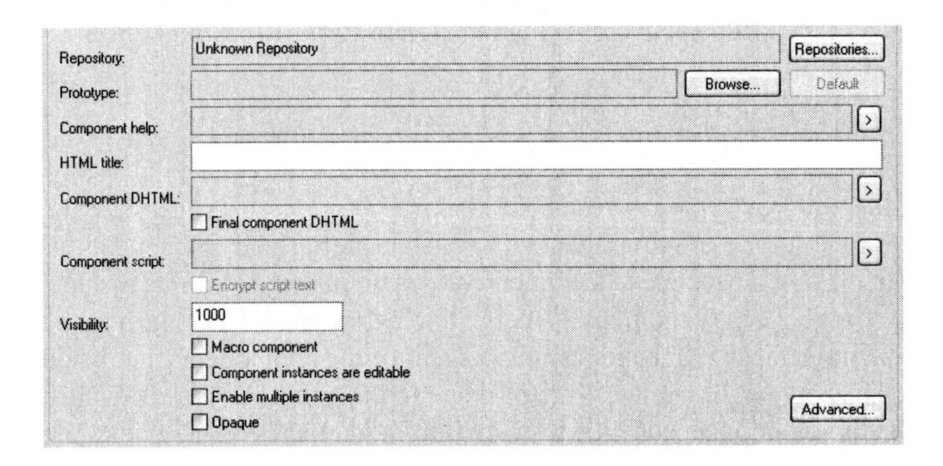

Figure 7.6 The component-specific properties.

The **Repository** property indicates the repository that is to store files included in the component. Clicking the **Repositories** button will list all of the available repositories to select from, including new repository objects that were just created in the same SLD file.

The **Prototype** property specifies a component whose functionality this component will be based on. Any component can be specified as a prototype component; however, a circular relationship (one in which two components declare each other as prototypes) cannot exist. A component will inherit the specified prototype component's properties, resources, dependencies, and build process behavior. Because the prototype component can reference other prototype components, an inheritance chain can be created, such that all properties, resources, dependencies, and build process behaviors in the chain can be inherited by a component. For components that do not specify a prototype component, a default prototype component, which is supplied by each platform, will be used.

Additional help and/or configuration details can be included with a component by creating an HTML help file and specifying the file in the **Component help** property. The browse button to the right of the property is used to select the help file. When a help file is included in a component, right-clicking on a component in any Target Designer or Component Database Manager list and selecting **Component Help** from the pop-up menu will open a new window with the HTML component help file. The text entered in the **HTML title** property will appear in the title bar of the component help window.

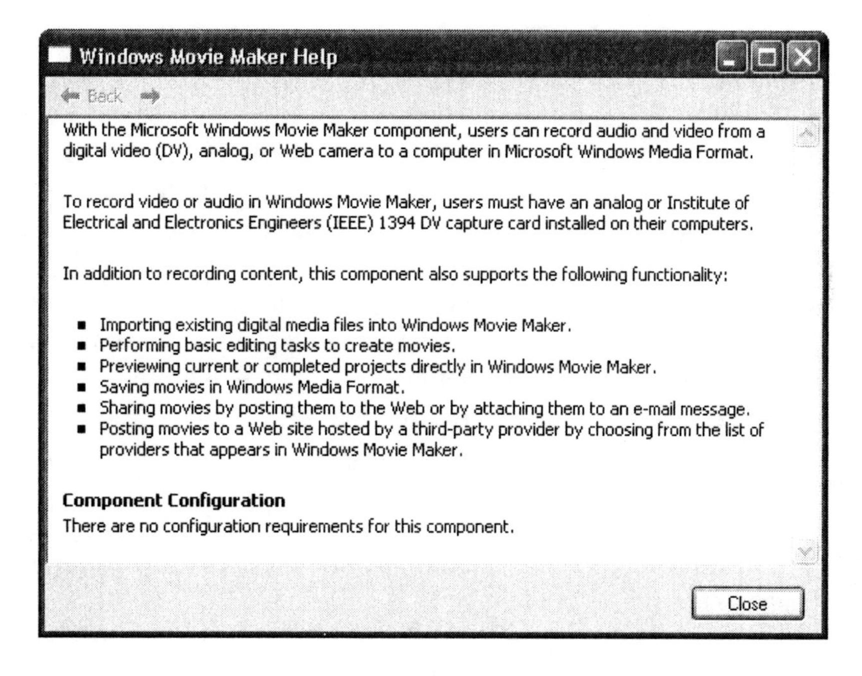

Figure 7.7 The Component help window displays additional help for a component.

When a DHTML file is specified in the **Component DHTML** property, the component will include user-configurable settings. The DHTML Active Server Page will appear in the details pane of Target Designer when component **Settings** is selected in the configuration editor. The source file specified in the **Component script** property can contain script text used by the **Component DHTML** Active Server Page.

Target Designer uses the **Visibility** property of components to control the display of components. Recall from the Target Designer chapter that the visibility threshold can be set in the **Options** window so that components of a visibility level less than the visibility threshold will not be displayed in the component browser. If required, such components will be automatically added during a dependency check. The default visibility level of a newly created component is 1000. It can be changed, but Microsoft recommends that this value be left as it is.

The remaining component-specific properties are check boxes. A check in the **Macro component** check box indicates that this component is a macro component. Recall from the Target Designer chapter that a macro component creates dependencies on individual components, which enables a collection of components to be added to a configuration simply by adding the macro component. Checking the **Component instances are editable** check box indicates that the component can be configured in Target Designer when it is added to the configuration. Configuration changes made to the component in Target Designer will not affect the component as it exists in the component database. Checking **Enable multiple instances** allows the component to be included more than once in a run-time image configuration. Checking **Opaque** will prevent the component's resources from being viewed in the Target Designer component browser.

Out of all of the objects that can be created in Component Designer, the component object has the most properties. Component objects also have several types of resources that can be added.

Section 7.5.2 Group Memberships

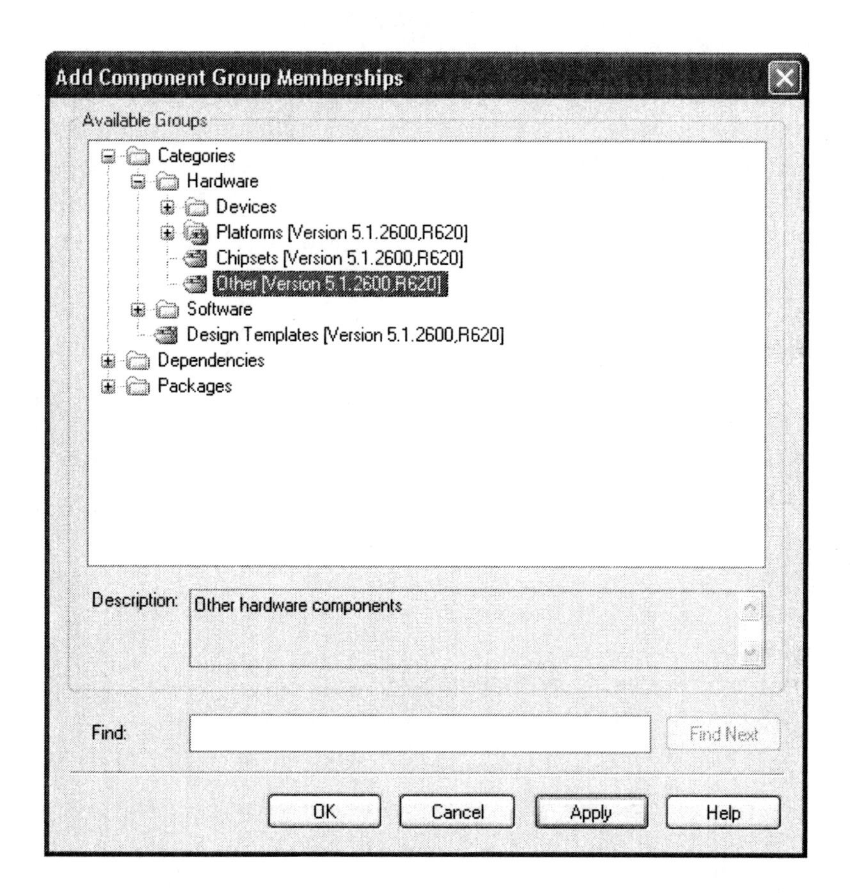

Figure 7.8 A component can be added as a member of multiple groups.

The component database can organize components and repositories in groups. Recall that group memberships are determined by the objects that claim membership to the group through a group membership resource, not by the groups themselves. The types of groups that repositories can be a part of were mentioned earlier. A component can be a member of any number of Category, Package, and/or Dependency groups. Assigning a **Category** group membership determines where the component will appear in the component browser tree of Target

Designer. A component may logically fall under more than one category of components. **Packages** group together functionally-related components and repositories. Grouping several components into a package enables the Component Database Manager to treat all of the package members as one unit, in particular when it comes to deleting or upgrading the objects. When a component is a member of a **Dependency** group, it means that if some other component has a dependency on that dependency group, the component will be one of the members of the dependency group which can satisfy the service requirements of the dependent component. Dependency groups will be covered in more detail later in the chapter.

Section 7.5.3 Files

During a run-time image build, Target Designer determines the files that are to be included by examining the file resources of the configuration's components. Any number of file resources can be added to a component.

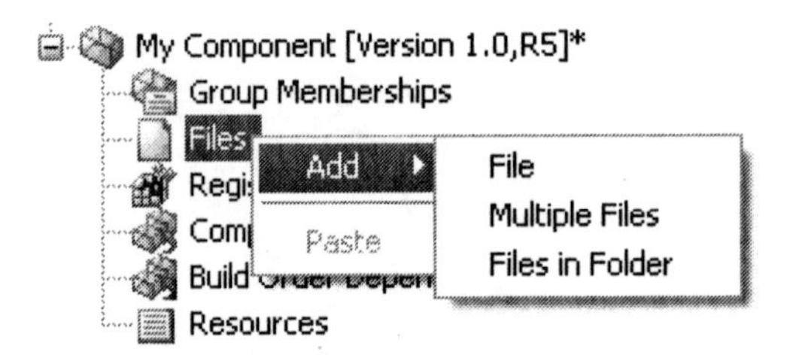

Figure 7.9 Adding Files in Component Designer.

To add files to a component in Component Designer, right click on **Files** and select **Add**. There are three ways to add file resources to a component in Component Designer. Selecting **Files in Folder** from the **Add** menu will prompt you to select a folder on your hard disk and all the files in that folder will be added to the component. Selecting **Multiple Files** will bring up a file browser that will allow you to select more than one file at a time. Selecting **File** from the **Add** menu will bring up the **Add Component File Resource** window, which contains the file resource properties. The same window is used to edit the properties of a file resource that has already been added to the component, only it is labeled **Edit Component File Resource** in the title bar.

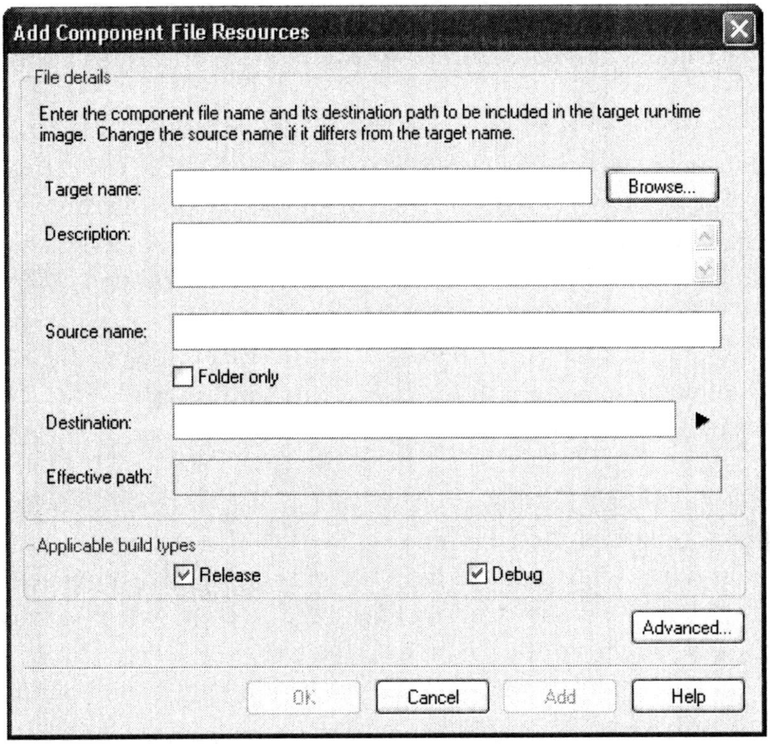

Figure 7.10 This window is used to modify a component's file properties.

Each file resource included in a component has its own specific properties which Target Designer reads during a run-time image build. The **Target name** property indicates the name that the file will take when it is built into the target's run-time image. If you want to use the original file name and don't want it to change after it is built into the run-time image, the **Browse** button enables you to browse through your local file system so you can copy the original name of the file into this field. A brief description of the file may be added in the **Description** property.

The **Source name** is the name of the actual file that will be copied from the repository into the run-time image. If this field is left blank, Component Designer assumes that the source name is the same as the target name. If the target name is to be different than the source name, then the name of the original file as it exists on the development system *must* be entered in this field. The source file's path should *not* be entered because all files are copied from repositories during an OS build.

The **Destination** property indicates the folder where the file will reside in the run-time image. The destination is an effective path. Component Designer uses directory identifiers, or *DIRIDs*, to specify the effect path. A DIRID is a number that represents a path on the system. For example, %11% represents C:\Windows\system32\, and %24% represents the system root, C:\. A list of DIRIDs appears when you click the arrow button. If the desired folder does not exist in the list, it is recommended that one of the DIRIDs be used in specifying a destination path, for example, %24%\MyFolder\.

The **Effective path** is a read-only property which displays the full destination path and file name. For informational purposes, the path selected in the destination property is converted to display the full path and file name. Component Designer is not able to determine the root drive of the target system, which is why the development system's root drive appears in the effective path. The effective path name is localized for the target system when the run-time image is built. For example, an effective path of C:\Windows on the local system would be D:\Windows on the target device run-time image if the Target Designer configuration settings indicate that the image is to run on the D: drive.

In the **Applicable build types** property, you can specify if the file is to be included in a Debug build only, or a Release build only, or both. By default, both check boxes are selected so that the file will be copied into both a Release build and a Debug build.

Selecting the **Folder only** check box indicates that the file resource will create only the folder specified in the Destination property. The **Target name** and **Source name** properties will be grayed-out and empty, indicating that no files will be added, and the **Effective path** field will display only the folder in the **Destination** property.

Section 7.5.4 Registry Data

The registry is a hierarchical database used to store information necessary to configure the system for users, applications, and devices. Registry keys and values are organized in a tree structure similar to the way that folders and files are organized in the file system. In the file system, folders can contain other folders as well as files. In the registry, registry keys can contain other keys as well as values. Hence, registry keys are like file system folders.

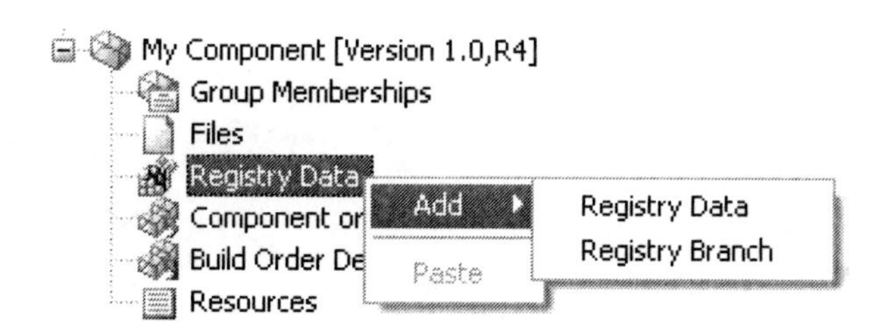

Figure 7.11 Adding Registry Data.

To add registry data to a component, there are two methods to select from. Right clicking on **Registry Data** and selecting **Add** will present you with the two options. Selecting the first option, **Registry Data**, will bring up the registry data properties dialog, which will enable you to manually enter the registry data. Selecting the second option, **Registry Branch** as the registry adding method, will bring up a browser which will enable you to browse the registry of your local machine and copy a registry key, along with all its sub-keys and values, from your development machine's registry to your component. If the component is going to include a set of registry data that the Windows operating system uses, this is a convenient way to include all of the registry data located under a key without having to manually create a registry key's tree structure by individually entering every registry key and value required.

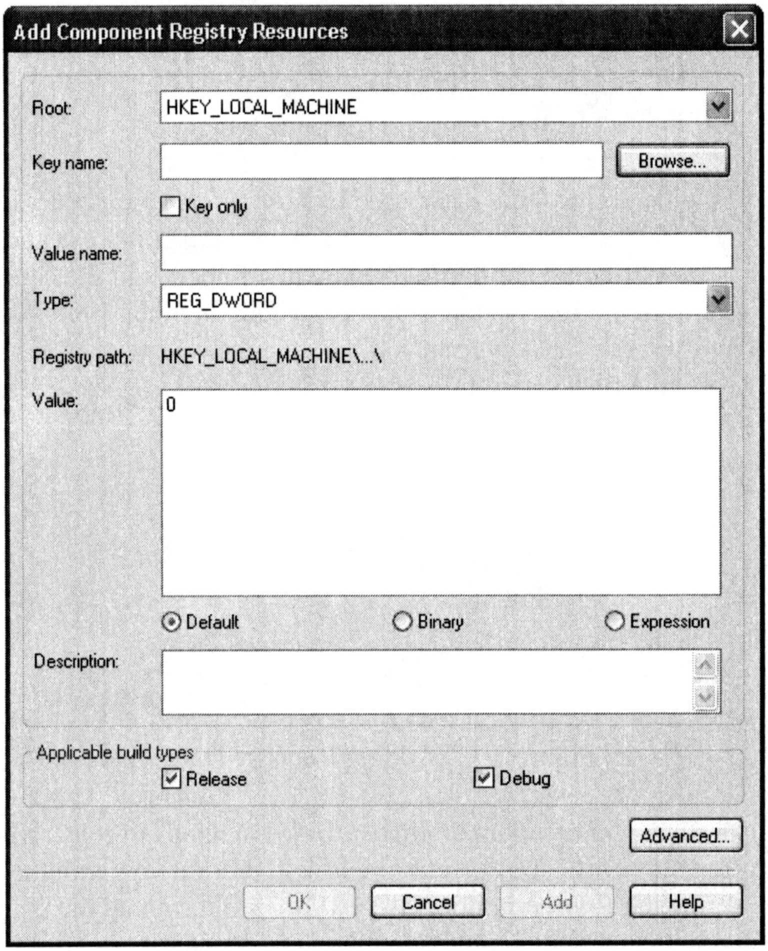

Figure 7.12 The property page for registry data.

The registry data properties dialog appears when you add registry data or select the properties of registry data that has already been added to a component. This dialog box is common to both Component Designer and Target Designer. Each registry resource has the following properties:

The **Root** pull-down menu lists the roots for all registry data. All registry data falls under one of the root keys. The **Key** field is used to specify the registry path for the sub-key that is to be created under the selected root key. Since the root of the sub-key is already specified in the **Root** property, the root key does not need to be included in the path of the **Key** property. Registry keys can be manually entered, or you can click the **Browse** button to browse the local development system registry for a key or value to copy into the registry resource. If a key is selected, then the root of the key will be automatically selected from the **Root** property and the full registry path of the key will be filled into the **Key** property. Checking the **Key only** check box will create the registry key without a value. If a value is selected from the browse dialog, the value's properties will be copied into the fields of the registry resource. In addition to the **Root** and **Key** properties being filled in, the **Value name**, **Type**, and **Value** properties will be filled in with those of the selected registry value. All of the properties mentioned can be manually entered if you choose to not use the browse feature. The read-only **Registry path** property displays the full path, complete with the registry root, for informational purposes only.

The type of data entered in the **Value** field is determined either by the selected data type from the **Type** pull-down menu and/or one of the selected radio buttons right below the **Value** field. If **Binary** is selected, data entered in the **Value** field is expected to be in binary (01100111b) or hexadecimal (0xB9E5) format, regardless of what is selected in the **Type** property. With **Expression** selected, data in the form of an expression, such as =**CurVal-1** is acceptable for the **Value** field.

Providing a description of the registry resource in the **Description** property is optional. In the **Applicable build types** property you can specify if the registry resource is to be included in a Debug build only, or a Release build only, or both. By default, both check boxes are selected so that the registry resource will be created for both a Release build and a Debug build.

The **Advanced** button brings up the Advanced Properties dialog box. In the Advanced Properties dialog box, Extended Properties and the Build Order can be modified. There is also a pull-down menu which has a selection of write options. One of the following write options can be selected:

- Always write the value.
- Write only if a value already exists.
- Write only if there is no existing value.
- Delete the key or value.
- Always edit the value.
- Edit only if a value already exists.

The last two write options listed involve editing a value. If selected, the data in the registry resource **Value** property is appended to the existing registry value data based on the data type. If the data type is REG_SZ or REG_EXPAND_SZ, then the text is concatenated. If the type is REG_MULTI_SZ, then the string is added to the multi-string. If the type is REG_DWORD, then a logical OR operation is performed. If the data is of any other type, including REG_BINARY, binary data is concatenated to the existing data.

Section 7.5.5 Component or Group Dependency

A component may require an association with one or more components. This can be done with the inclusion of a dependency. A dependency is a functional relationship between two or more components. A *component* dependency creates a relationship between one component and another component. A *group* dependency creates a relationship between one component and a group of components.

Including a component dependency in a component definition indicates that the component either requires a particular component or conflicts with a particular component. A group dependency indicates that the component is dependent upon a dependency group. A dependency group has a number of components as members. When a component is dependent upon a dependency group, the type of dependency relationship can be selected from the **Add Group Dependencies** dialog. For example, a component may require exactly one of the components in the selected dependency group to satisfy its service requirements, it may require at least one, or all, of the group's components, or it may conflict with components in the group. Another option is to use the default dependency rule that is established by the group.

Section 7.5.6 Build Order Dependency

A dependency which requires one component to include or exclude another component or group of components is known as an *include* dependency. The other type of dependency, known as a *build order* dependency, requires that during the build process, one component is processed either before or after another component. Typically, a build order dependency would be used to edit a registry key created by another component or to overwrite a file included by another component. Build order dependencies only specify the relative order that components are processed during the build process if the specified components are present. They do not include or exclude components.

A build order dependency can be either a *component build order* dependency, which requires that a specified component be built before or after a particular component, or a *group build order* dependency, which requires that all of the components of the specified group be built before or after a particular component.

Section 7.5.7 Resources

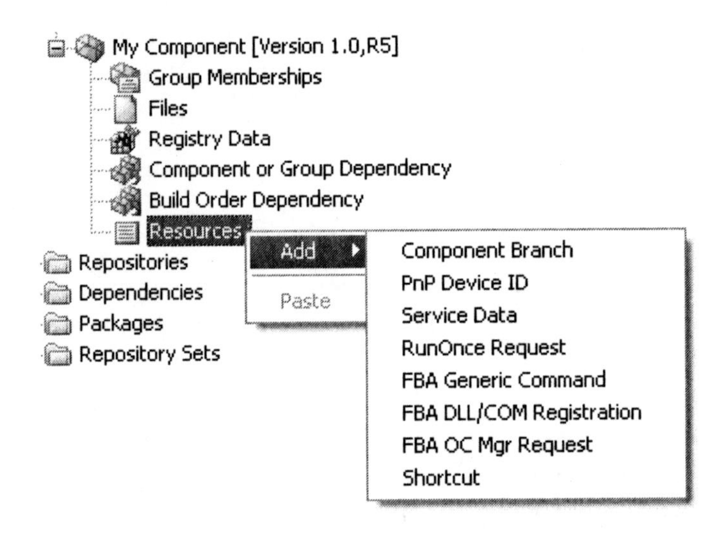

Figure 7.13 Adding component resources.

In addition to all of the types of resources that have been described so far, including files, registry data, and dependencies, a component can include other resources. Each of these additional resources contain a set of pre-defined extended properties that represent some specific processing required during the build process. The additional resources are described below. Appendix A lists and describes the pre-defined extended properties for each of the resources.

A component can become obsolete during the life of an embedded system. When a component becomes obsolete, it must be prevented from being included in a configuration. At the same time, there may be one or more existing components in an existing configuration that have a dependency on the obsolete component, so it can not be deleted from the database. When a component reaches this stage, Component Designer provides a way to mark the component as End-Of-Life (EOL). A **Component Branch** resource can be included in an EOL component to specify a replacement component or components. A branch resource specifies the version of the replacement component using the Version Independent GUID (VIGUID).

Optionally, you can change the minimum required revision for the replacement component.

Plug and Play (PnP) is a combination of hardware and software support that enables a computer system to recognize and adapt to hardware configuration changes with little or no intervention by a user. The **PnP Device ID** resource is used to annotate a component with Plug and Play information for Plug and Play device drivers. Target Analyzer gathers identifiers of the hardware devices on the target system into a results file. When the results file is imported into Target Designer or Component Designer, the hardware components of a target system are determined by matching the identifiers listed in the results file with PnP Device ID resources of hardware components in the component database. During the build process, Target Designer uses the PnP Device ID resources of devices in the configuration that are critical in booting the system, such as disk controllers and system bus drivers, to populate the registry with information needed at boot time. The PnP Device ID resource is created automatically when an INF file is imported into Component Designer, so it should not be added manually.

A *service* is an application type that runs in the background. A service performs a specific system function to support other programs, particularly at low (close to hardware) level. Components that define a Windows service require a **Service Data** resource. The extended property values of a Service Data resource correspond to the parameters passed to the **CreateService** Windows API, although **CreateService** is not actually used to process this resource type.

A program can be specified to execute upon the very first boot or after every logon by adding a **RunOnce Request** resource to a component. The RunOnce Request uses the following Windows XP registry entries:

- HKEY_LOCAL_MACHINE\SOFTWARE\Microsoft\CurrentVersion\Run
- HKEY_LOCAL_MACHINE\SOFTWARE\Microsoft\CurrentVersion\RunOnce

- HKEY_LOCAL_MACHINE\SOFTWARE\Microsoft\CurrentVersion\RunOnceEx

When the Explorer shell is included in the run-time image, the *Run* key is processed by the Explorer shell after every logon. If a shell other than the Explorer shell is used instead, the *Run* key is processed by the First Boot Agent. Even after the first boot, the FBA will always process the *Run* key when the Explorer shell is not present.

The *RunOnce* key is processed by the FBA during the very first boot of the run-time image. It is processed following Plug and Play device enumeration and then again following DLL registration. After that, it is then processed after logon, exactly like the *Run* key is processed, but it will not happen again on logons that follow.

The *RunOnceEx* key is processed only by the Explorer shell after logon. If the Explorer shell is not present in the run-time image, this key is ignored.

The **FBA Generic Command** resource launches a specified program during the first boot of the run-time image. The First Boot Agent calls the Win32 **CreateProcess** API to run a program and pass any command line arguments.

The **FBA DLL/COM Registration** resource is used to register a Component Object Model (COM) InProc server during the first boot of the run-time image. The FBA calls the Win32 function LoadLibrary and then optionally calls DllRegisterServer/DllUnregisterServer and/or DllInstall. In addition to listing and describing the extended properties of this resource, Appendix A also has a table to help clarify how the various combinations of *Flags*, *DllInstall*, and *DllRegister* properties are interpreted.

The **FBA OC Mgr Request** resource is the Optional Component Manager, which allows the integration of external components into the setup process. This directive enables you to specify setup routines your component would normally run during a Windows XP setup.

The component database has a component called Standard Start Menu Shortcuts which will add some commonly used shortcuts to the Start menu of the Explorer shell. If you wish to create your own custom shortcuts, Component Designer enables you to create your own shortcut on the Start menu, desktop, or wherever you want to put it in the file system. Simply add a **Shortcut** resource and fill in the appropriate properties. In addition to the properties, whatever is typed into the Shortcut resource's description field will appear when you right-click the shortcut in the run-time image and then choose **Properties**.

Section 7.6 Dependencies

The earlier discussion about component dependencies should have made clear that a component can have dependencies on a single component or on a group of components such that one or more members of the group would satisfy the service requirements of the component. Also recall that a component can be a member of any of three types of groups: categories, packages, and dependency groups. There are several pre-defined dependency groups. For example, there is a Shell dependency group whose membership list includes all of the available shells, such as the Explorer shell, Command Shell, etc. Any component that has a dependency on the Shell dependency group, such as the Windows Logon component, will require that exactly one of the Shell dependency group's members be added to the configuration.

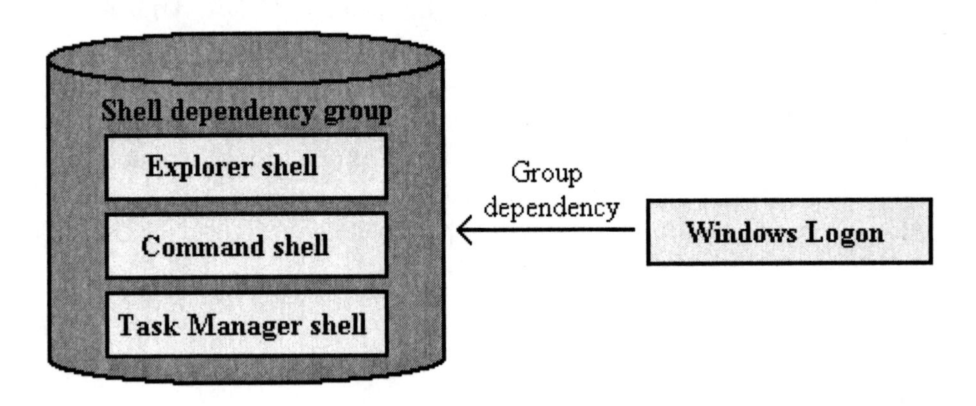

Figure 7.14 Use of the Shell dependency group as an example of a dependency group.

Component Designer enables you to create your own dependency group. As with any other group, membership to the dependency group is determined by the members. A dependency group has the same type of properties as the repository set and package objects (typical object properties such as Name and Vendor, platform, etc), but it has one property that the other two do not have. The Default Dependency Type property enables you to select the default type of dependency that the group will have. One of the choices below can be selected as the group's default dependency type, such that any component dependent on this group:

- Requires exactly one component from the group
- Requires one or more component(s) from the group
- Requires zero or one component from the group
- Requires all components from the group

or

- Conflicts with components in the group.

The Shell dependency group, for example, has the default dependency type such that any component dependent on the Shell dependency group requires exactly one component from the group.

In the following exercise, you are going to create a new application component for Microsoft Paint. First, you will perform some setup steps for this exercise, including creating new folders, copying mspaint.exe to your working directory, and creating an HTML sample component help file. Then you will use Component Designer to create objects in an SLD file. Then, in Exercise 9, you will test the component in a run-time image build.

Section 7.7 EXERCISE 8

Set up for this exercise

1. Open **My Computer** from the **Start** menu.

2. Browse to the **C:\XPE dev** folder that was created previously and create the following two subfolders:

   MyMSPaint SLD *For the SLD file created by Component Designer.*

   MyMSPaint SLD\Rep *For the files associated with the component.*

3. Browse to the folder **C:\Windows\System32**, locate the file **mspaint.exe**, and copy it to the folder **C:\XPE dev\MyMSPaint SLD\Rep**.

4. A component help file, **MyMSPaintHelp.html**, has already been created and exists on the accompanying CD. It can be copied from the CD to the folder **C:\XPE dev\MyMSPaint SLD\Rep**, or you can type the following into a text editor:

```
<html>
<head>
```

```
<title>My MSPaint Application</title>
</head>
<body bgcolor="#FFFFFF" text="#000000">
<hr>
<b><u>About MyMsPaint:</u></b><br>
This program is a copy of the Microsoft MsPaint application.
This copy was made to demonstrate the creation of an application
component using Component Designer.
</body>
</html>
```

Create a new System Level Definition (SLD) file

1. Open Component Designer. Click on the **Start** menu, select **All Programs**, then select **Microsoft Windows Embedded Studio**, and click on **Component Designer**.

2. Select **Options** from the **Tools** menu.

3. On the **Object Defaults** tab, click on **Auto-fill each new object with these defaults when created**, fill in your default information, and then click the **OK** button.

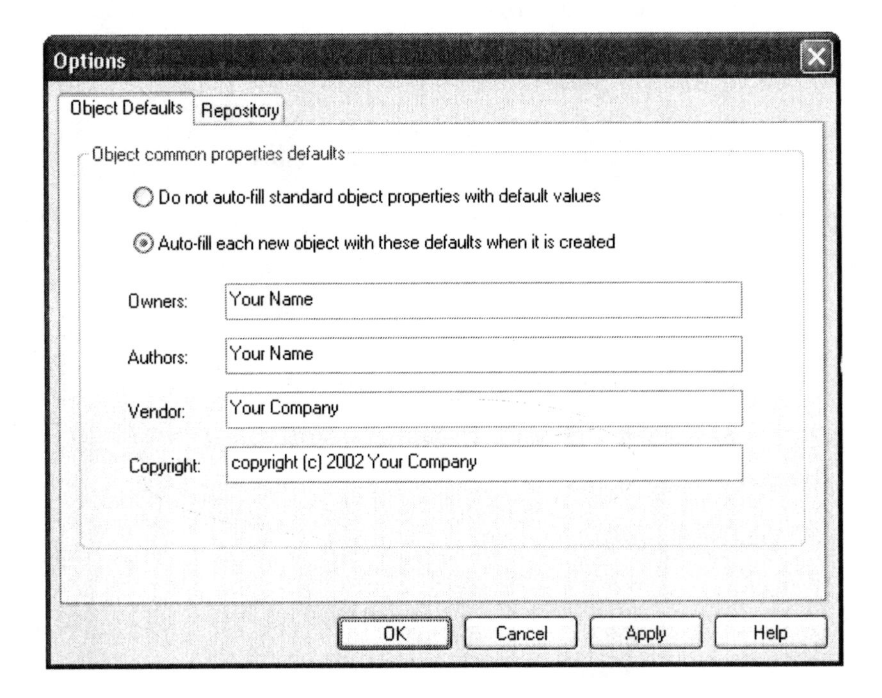

Figure 7.15 The auto-fill option for creating new objects.

Note: The previous two steps are not mandatory in order to have a working object. However, using the auto-fill feature will spare you from having to fill in these particular properties for every object you create in Component Designer.

4. From the **File** menu, select **New**.

5. From the **File** menu, select **Save As**, then save the file as **MyMSPaint.sld** in the folder **C:\XPE dev\MyMSPaint SLD**.

Create a new package object

Note: Creating a package will serve for demonstration purposes of the use of packages. After this exercise, you can make other component and repository objects members of this package, whether created from exercises in this book or your own practice exercises. You can delete the package in Component Database Manager (which will delete all of the package's members) if you no longer want the practice exercise objects in your database.

1. In the SLD browser, expand the **Windows Embedded Client (x86)** folder.

2. Right-click on the **Packages** folder and select **Add Package**.

3. In the **Name** property, name the package **Component Designer Exercises**.

4. In the **Description** property type:

```
This package contains the component and repository objects that
were created for exercises.
```

Create a new repository object

1. In the SLD browser, right-click on the **Repositories** folder and select **Add Repository**.

2. In the **Name** property, name the repository **MyMSPaint Repository**.

3. In the **Description** property type:

```
This repository was created for the mspaint.exe application and
the MyMSPaintHelp.html component help file.
```

4. To the right of the **Source Path** property, click the **Browse** button.

5. Browse to select the folder **C:\XPE dev\MyMSPaint SLD\Rep**, and then click the **OK** button.

Note: Every file in this folder will be copied to the new repository that is created by Component Database Manager when this SLD file is imported.

6. Right-click on **MyMSPaint Repository** and select **Add Group Membership**.

7. In the **Add Repository Group Membership** window, expand the **Packages** folder if it is not already expanded, and select the **Component Designer Exercises** package, which will probably be located at the bottom of the list. Click the **OK** button when finished.

Create a new component object

1. In the SLD browser, right-click on the **Components** folder and select **Add Component**.

2. In the **Name** property, name the component **My MSPaint**.

3. In the **Description** property, type:

```
The MyMSPaint application is a copy of Microsoft's mspaint.exe
application. It will automatically be launched after every
login.
```

4. To specify a repository, click on the **Repositories** button to the right of the **Repository** property.

5. Select the **MyMSPaint Repository** from the list, and then click the **OK** button.

6. To specify a component help file, click the right arrow (>) button to the right of the **Component help** property and select **Browse**.

7. Browse to the folder **C:\XPE dev\MyMSPaint SLD\Rep**, select **MyM-SPaintHelp.html**, and then click the **Open** button.

8. In the **HTML title** property, type **My MSPaint**.

Add the file reference to the component object

1. In the SLD browser under the **My MSPaint** component, right-click on **Files**, select **Add**, and then click on **Files**.

2. For the **Target name** property, type **mymspaint.exe**.

3. For the **Source name** property, type **mspaint.exe**.

Note: Notice that no path is needed in the Source name property. During the build process, Target Designer will copy the file mspaint.exe from the repository specified for this component to the build destination folder, where it will be renamed mymspaint.exe.

4. To specify the directory where the file will reside in the run-time image, click on the right arrow button (>) to the right of the **Destination** property.

5. Select **%11%** from the list. The parameter %11% is a DIRID that represents the directory \Windows\System32.

6. Click the **OK** button.

Add registry data to the component

1. In the SLD browser under the **My MSPaint** component, right-click on **Registry Data**, select **Add**, and then click on **Registry Data**. The **Add Component Registry Resources** window will appear.

2. To the right of the **Key name** property, click the **Browse** button.

Note: This browse feature enables you to copy a registry path from your local system registry if the registry data you wish to include in your component already exists on the development system. In this case, you are adding registry data that enables the Windows operating system to automatically launch a specified program.

3. Under the root key **HKEY_CURRENT_USER**, browse to and select the registry folder **Software\Microsoft\Windows\CurrentVersion\Run**, then click the **OK** button.

4. In the **Value name** property, type **MYMSPAINT**.

5. In the **Type** property, select **REG_SZ** from the pull-down menu.

6. In the **Value** property, type **mymspaint.exe**.

7. Click the **OK** button.

Add component dependencies

1. In the SLD browser under the **My MSPaint** component, right-click on **Component or Group Dependency**, select **Add**, and then click on **Component Dependency**.

2. Because the component contains registry data that causes it to be automatically launched upon login, create an include dependency on the Registry Editor component by double-clicking on the **Registry Editor** component, which is located under **Software : System : User Interface : Shells : Windows Shell**.

3. The Windows Accessories component is a component that includes applications such as Notepad, Wordpad, and Mspaint, to name a few. The My MSPaint component will only include a copy of the Mspaint application, but it will rely on some of the same dependencies that the Windows Accessories component relies on. Create an include dependency on the Windows Accessories component by double-clicking on **Windows Accessories**, which is located under **Software : System : User Interface : Shells : Windows Shell**.

4. Click the **Cancel** button to close the window.

Add two shortcut resources

1. The first shortcut resource will create a shortcut on the desktop for the mymspaint application. In the SLD browser under the **My MSPaint** component, right-click on **Resources**, select **Add**, and then click on **Shortcut**.

2. The Extended Properties can be modified individually by clicking on a property in the **Extended Properties** list and clicking on the **Edit** button. Make the following modifications to the Extended Properties listed below:

Extended Property Name	Change Value To:
DstName	Shortcut to MyMSPaint.lnk
DstPath	%16409%
IconLocation	mymspaint.exe,0
TargetPath	%11%\mymspa~1.exe
WorkDir	%11%

Note: The TargetPath property requires file names to be in the DOS 8.3 format, which is why mymspaint.exe needs to be typed in as mymspa~1.exe.

3. Click the **OK** button.

4. The second shortcut resource will create a shortcut on the desktop for the regedt32 application, so that you can access the registry in order to remove the key that automatically launches MyMSPaint. In the SLD browser under the **My MSPaint** component, right-click on **Resources**, select **Add**, and then click on **Shortcut**.

5. Make the following modifications to the Extended Properties listed below:

Extended Property Name	Change Value To:
DstName	Shortcut to Regedt32.lnk
DstPath	%16409%

Extended Property Name	Change Value To:
IconLocation	regedt32.exe,0
TargetPath	%11%\regedt32.exe
WorkDir	%11%

6. Click the **OK** button.

Add group memberships

1. In the SLD browser under the **My MSPaint** component, right-click on **Group Memberships** and click on **Add Group Membership** to add the **Software : System : User Interface : Applications** category group membership:

   a. Click the + on the left side of a node in the **Available groups** list to expand the node and view its child nodes. Expand the **Categories** root node, and then expand the **Software**, **System**, and **User Interface** nodes.

   b. Click the **Applications** group and then click the **OK** button.

2. Right-click on **Group Memberships** and click on **Add Group Membership** to add the **Software : Applications : Other** category group membership:

   a. Click the + on the left side of a node in the **Available groups** list to expand the node and view its child nodes. Expand the **Categories** root node, expand the **Software** node, and then expand the **Applications** node.

   b. Click the **Other** group and then click the **OK** button.

3. Right-click on **Group Memberships** and click on **Add Group Membership** to add the **Component Designer Exercises** package group membership:

   a. Click the + on the left side of a node in the **Available groups** list to expand the node and view its child nodes. Expand the **Packages** root node.

b. Click the **Component Designer Exercises** group and then click the **OK** button.

4. Save the SLD file and exit Component Designer.

Section 7.8 EXERCISE 9

Use Component Database Manager to import the SLD file into the component database and verify the creation of the Component Designer objects

1. Open Component Database Manager. Click on the **Start** menu, select **All Programs**, then select **Microsoft Windows Embedded Studio**, and click on **Component Database Manager**.

2. On the **Database** tab, click the **Import** button.

3. When the **Import SLD** window appears, click on the ellipsis button [...] to select the SLD file to import.

4. Browse to the folder **C:\XPE dev\MyMSPaint SLD**, select the file **MyMSPaint.sld**, and then click the **Open** button.

5. Click the **Import** button, and then click the **Close** button after the import process is complete.

6. To verify that the package and the component have been inserted into the database:

   a. Click on the **Component** tab.

   b. Under the **Choose a package** property, select the **Component Designer Exercises** package.

   c. Verify that the component **My MSPaint** component is in the component list.

7. To verify that the repository was created:

   a. Click the **Repository** tab.

   b. Verify that the **MyMSPaint Repository** object is in the list of **Available repositories**.

   c. Open **My Computer** from the **Start** menu and browse to the folder indicated in the repository's **Location** field. Verify that the appropriate files are present in the directory.

8. Click the **Close** button to close Component Database Manager.

Test the component in a run-time image build

1. Open Target Designer. Click on the **Start** menu, select **All Programs**, then select **Microsoft Windows Embedded Studio**, and click on **Target Designer**.

2. Click **Open** on the **File** menu and browse to the folder **C:\XPE dev\TA_DATA**.

3. Assuming that you successfully completed the Target Designer exercise, select **TAPBASE.slx** and click the **Open** button.

4. In the Component Browser, add the **My MSPaint** component from **Software : Applications : Other**.

5. In the Configuration Editor, double-click the **User Interface Core** component to expand it, and then click on **Settings**.

6. In the Details Pane, click on the checkbox labeled **Show desktop icons** so that a check appears.

7. Perform dependency check by selecting **Check Dependencies** from the **Configuration** menu.

8. Click the **Close** button when the dependency check is complete.

9. Build the run-time image by selecting **Build Target Image** from the **Configuration** menu.

10. If it is not already done, set the **Destination** folder as **C:\Windows Embedded Images**, then click the **Build** button. If prompted to perform a dependency check, click **No**. If prompted to delete the contents of the **Destination** folder, click **Yes**.

11. After the build process completes, click the **Close** button.

12. Save the configuration and close Target Designer.

13. Open **My Computer** from the **Start** menu and format the D: drive as **FAT**.

14. Copy the entire contents of the folder **C:\Windows Embedded Images** to **D:**.

15. Make sure that the boot.ini file is set up for dual booting. If this has not been done, refer to Exercise 6 in the Target Designer chapter.

16. Reboot the system into Windows XP Embedded.

17. After the FBA successfully completes, the mymspaint.exe application should be launched and the desktop should have the MyMSPaint and Regedt32 shortcuts.

This chapter has covered all of the features of Component Designer, the main component authoring tool for Windows XP embedded components. Every object that can be created in component designer was discussed: Repositories, Repository Sets, Packages, Components, and Dependencies. The properties of each object type were described, as well as the different types of resources that can be added to components and repositories. Exercise 8 demonstrated the use of Component Designer to create database objects, including a package, a repository, and a component. The repository included a group membership resource, which made it a member of the package that was created. The component included package and category group memberships, a file, registry data, dependencies, and shortcut resources. Exercise 9 demonstrated the use of Component Database Manager to import the newly created SLD file and verify that the database objects were created. The component was then tested by including it into a Target Designer configuration which was created in the previous chapter.

The next chapter will cover the Embedded Enabling Features of Windows XP Embedded.

CHAPTER 8 Embedded Enabling Features

Up to this point, the four main tools (Component Database Manager, Target Analyzer, Target Designer, and Component Designer) have been described and used in creating run-time images. Except for the First Boot Agent, the features that were built into the run-time image are features that were inherited from the desktop version of Windows XP (a shell, device drivers, applications, etc.). Window XP Embedded includes embedded enabling features to assist in customizing the operating system for different embedded device scenarios. Embedded enabling features are specific to the Windows XP Embedded operating system, and are the subjects of this chapter.

Section 8.1 Shell Customization

A shell is an application that serves as the primary interface between the user and the system. The shell is responsible for loading and executing applications. There are three pre-defined shells provided by Windows XP Embedded.

The **Explorer shell** is nearly identical to the shell that desktop Windows operating systems use. It has a task bar, start menu, and a desktop. There are several components that enable you to customize the appearance and behavior of this shell, but they are not automatically included in the image as dependencies when you include the Explorer shell in the configuration. For example, you will need to include the *Date/Time Control Panel* component in order to be able to change the date and time displayed on the task bar, and you must make modifications to the *User Interface Core* component settings in order to include items in the Start menu. Most of these components can be found in the Target Designer component browser under the category **Software : System : User Interface : Shells : Windows Shell**.

When the **Command shell** is used, the system uses a command window as the shell. There is no desktop, start menu, or task bar. If this shell is to be used, it is recommended that you also include the **Misc. Command Line Tools** component, which is located under the category **Software : System : System Services : Base** in the Target Designer component browser. It contains the shutdown.exe application so you can shut down your system.

The **Task Manager shell** displays only the Task Manager as the shell. Using the Task Manager you can perform several tasks, such as launching, ending, or switching between applications, ending a process, and monitoring performance.

Additionally, a custom shell can be created so that the system uses a specified application as the shell. The Explorer shell launches the application *explorer.exe*, the Command shell launches *cmd.exe*, and the Task Manager shell launches *taskmgr.exe* as the primary user interface. A custom shell will launch a specified application as the primary user interface. This chapter contains an exercise that will step you through the creation of a custom shell component using an existing application as the shell. Information on creating a custom shell application can be found in the Windows SDK and DDK documentation.

Section 8.2 Headless Operation

The term "headless system" refers to a system that has no Video Graphics Adapter (VGA) card, keyboard, or mouse. An example of a headless system would be a Network Attached Storage device that has a very dedicated role. The Windows XP operating system requires a video driver in order for graphics subsystem function calls to communicate with the hardware. All of the currently available video drivers rely on the underlying hardware. However, to support headless operation, Windows XP Embedded includes a headless VGA driver that eliminates the need for video hardware. The graphics subsystem can make function calls to the driver, but the driver does not access video hardware. Instead, video information is kept in memory and an acknowledgement is returned indicating successful completion of a video command.

The headless VGA driver can be included in the run-time image by including either the **Headless VGA Driver** component or the **Terminal Services Core** component. Both components include the headless VGA driver, but only one of the components can exist in a configuration. Adding terminal services significantly increases the size of the run-time image footprint. The run-time image still requires the **VGA Boot Driver** component to be included in the configuration, regardless whether or not a VGA card is present. The Target Designer visibility threshold in the Options window must be set to 200 or less in order to see the **VGA Boot Driver** component in the component browser.

Section 8.2.1 Headless Design Considerations

When building a headless system, there are a few things to consider. The BIOS must support the ability to run without a video adapter and/or keyboard. Some BIOSs will halt if these devices are not attached. To support a headless system, the BIOS should be able to turn off the detection of the video adapter and/or keyboard. Except for this issue, Windows XP Embedded has embedded enabling features that provide solutions for headless system scenarios. The features mentioned will be covered in more detail throughout the chapter.

One such solution is to include networking support in the system. Networking is not categorized an embedded enabling feature, but it can be used as an alternative user input method of operating a headless computer. An application that runs on a headless system can be programmed to accept user input over a network connection, or perhaps from an uploaded file. Networking can also be used in conjunction with some of the remote administration tools included in the embedded enabling features of Windows XP Embedded, such as the Telnet Server and Terminal Server Remote Desktop which can be used to operate the system remotely. The system does not necessarily have to be a headless system to take advantage of embedded enabling features like this, but it is often useful to have the ability to remotely access the system, headless or not, for administrative purposes.

Another potential obstacle to a headless system is the inability to directly respond to interactive message boxes, dialog boxes, and system messages. The Windows XP Embedded operating system can be set up to intercept these messages, respond with a default reply, and log the messages. This concept is called System Message Interception. You can also create a custom application for System Message Interception handling.

Section 8.3 Remote Management

For some device scenarios, such as a headless system, you may not be able to gain physical access to the system after it has been deployed. Windows XP Embedded provides a set of features to help administer such a device.

The **Telnet Server** enables users to connect to the device from another computer as Telnet clients and provides a command prompt user interface for operating the computer, just like the interface that the Command shell presents. By default, the Telnet Server uses the valid user name/password combinations on the local server to log on to the system.

Using the Telnet Server to remotely operate a system that uses the Command shell enables remote users to perform just about any task that can be performed when operating the system locally. If the remote system uses the Explorer shell, Telnet Server limits remote users to using command line applications. The **Terminal Server Remote Desktop** component provides remote access to the desktop of a computer that is running Terminal Services. When connected, the remote machine will have a window which displays the desktop of the XP Embedded target and allows you to perform operations on the target as if you were sitting right in front of it.

File Transfer Protocol (FTP) is one of the oldest protocols still in use. It was designed to move files between computers and handle the translation problems that may occur when different types of computers try to communicate. The **IIS FTP Server** component enables users to connect to the local server from a remote machine and transfer files between the machines on a network using TCP/IP, such as internet. FTP commands can also be used to work with files, such as listing files and folders on the remote system. Because the FTP service works with IIS, files can be transferred using a web browser.

In order to connect to a device and use the Telnet Server, Terminal Services Remote Desktop, or the IIS FTP Server, the password used to log on to the system cannot be an empty string or blank spaces. A password can be assigned to the Administrator account in a Target Designer configuration. Select the **Administrator Account** component, click the **Advanced** button in the Details pane, and edit the **cmiUserPassword** extended property to enter a password. The same can be done for any **User Account** components that exist in the configuration.

Also known as Web-Based Enterprise Management (WBEM), **Windows Management Instrumentation** (WMI) is a management infrastructure that provides managers with information and control in an enterprise environment. Using WMI, information can be queried and set on desktop systems, applications, networks, and other enterprise components. WMI capabilities can be built into monitoring applications that alert users when important incidents occur. WMI offers a variety of programming interfaces and tools that developers can use to further tailor their management applications. More information about WMI can be found in the Microsoft Platform SDK.

The **Simple Network Management Protocol** (SNMP) is the Internet standard protocol for exchanging management information between management console applications and managed entities. The managed entities can include hosts, routers, bridges, and hubs. SNMP can be used to monitor network performance and usage, configure remote devices, and detect network faults or inappropriate access. More information about SNMP can be found in the Microsoft Platform SDK.

In the next exercise, you will include remote management components into an existing run-time image and test the connection utilizing a separate remote computer on the local network. It is recommended that the remote computer run Windows XP Professional, but a Windows 2000 machine will work.

Section 8.4 EXERCISE 10

Include the components needed for remote management into an existing Target Designer configuration and build the run-time image

1. Open Target Designer. Click on the **Start** menu, select **All Programs**, then select **Microsoft Windows Embedded Studio**, and click on **Target Designer**.

2. Click **Open** on the **File** menu and browse to the folder **C:\XPE dev\TA_DATA**.

3. Assuming that the Target Designer exercise in Chapter 6 was successfully completed, select **TAPBASE.slx** and click the **Open** button.

4. From the **File** menu, select **Save As**.

5. In the **File name** text box, type **RemoteAdmin.slx** and then click the **Save** button.

6. Add the following components for Remote Management:

Component	Location
Telnet Server	Software : System : Management : Applications
Terminal Services Remote Desktop	Software : System : Management : Infrastructure
Basic TCP/IP Networking	Software : System : Networking & Communications
TCP/IP Utilities	Software : System : Networking & Communications : Applications
IIS FTP Server	Software : System : Networking & Communications : Infrastructure

7. (Optional) If your BIOS supports headless operation (i.e. can run without a VGA card) and you wish to make the device a headless system, remove the display adapter component from the configuration. The **Terminal Services Remote Desktop** component that you just added will include the **Terminal Services Core** component as a dependency during a dependency check with the auto-resolve dependencies feature enabled. The **Terminal Services Core** component includes the Headless VGA driver. A convenient way to find your display adapter component is to select the **Components** node in the configuration editor, click the **Category** heading in the details pane to sort the components by category, and browse the list for components with the category **Hardware : Devices : Display Adapters**.

8. In order to connect to the target and use the included remote management features, the user account cannot have an empty string for a password. To set a password for the Administrator account, select the **Administrator Account** component in the configuration editor, click the **Advanced** button in the Details pane, and edit **cmiUserPassword** in the **Extended Properties** list. Type in a password, for example, **admin**.

9. Add the **Automatic Logon** component, which is located under the category **Software : System : Security : Infrastructure**.

10. Expand the **Automatic Logon** component in the configuration editor, select **Settings**, and then, in the details pane, type **Administrator** in the **User name** property and type the password of the administrator account, **admin**, in the **Password** property.

11. Perform dependency check by selecting **Check Dependencies** from the **Configuration** menu.

12. Click the **Close** button when the dependency check is complete.

13. Build the run-time image by selecting **Build Target Image** from the **Configuration** menu.

14. If it is not already done, set the **Destination** folder as **C:\Windows Embedded Images**, then click the **Build** button. If prompted to perform a dependency check, click **No**. When prompted to delete the contents of the **Destination** folder, click **Yes**.

15. After the build process completes, click the **Close** button.

16. Save the configuration and close Target Designer.

17. Open **My Computer** from the **Start** menu and format the D: drive as **FAT**. WARNING! This will erase all data on D:!

18. Copy all of the *contents* of the folder **C:\Windows Embedded Images**, not the **Windows Embedded Images** folder itself, to **D:**.

19. Make sure that the boot.ini file is set up for a dual boot system. If this has not been done, refer to Exercise 6 of the Target Designer chapter.

20. Reboot the system into Windows XP Embedded.

Test the remote connection using the remote administration console applications, telnet and ftp

1. Wait for the First Boot Agent to successfully complete.

2. From a separate computer connected to the same network as the target device, establish a Telnet session with the Windows XP Embedded system by opening a command window on the remote system and typing **telnet target** at the command prompt. A command window can be opened by selecting **Run** from the **Start** menu and typing **cmd.exe**.

3. The Telnet server will prompt you for a user name and password. Type in **Administrator** for the user name and **admin** (or whatever password you assigned to the Administrator account) for the password.

4. Once connected, you can execute commands on the command line, such as listing directories or executing console applications. You can obtain the IP address of the target device, as well as other information about the network connection, by typing **ipconfig /all**.

5. Type **quit** at the Telnet command prompt on the remote machine to exit Telnet.

6. From the separate system, establish an FTP session with the Windows XP Embedded system by typing **ftp target** at the command prompt.

Note: The target device's IP address can be used in place of the computer name when establishing a remote connection to the target device.

7. The FTP server will prompt you for a user name and password. Type in **Administrator** for the user name and **admin** (or whatever password you assigned to the Administrator account) for the password.

8. Once connected, you can execute ftp commands at the ftp prompt, such as listing directories and files, changing directories, and, of course, transferring files. A list of ftp commands can be listed by typing **help** at the ftp prompt.

9. To disconnect from the ftp server, type **bye** at the ftp prompt.

Test the remote connection using the Remote Desktop Connection application

1. From a separate computer connected to the same network as the target device, establish a remote desktop session with the Windows XP Embedded system. If the separate computer is running Windows XP Professional, the Remote Desktop Connection application is included with the OS. It can be launched by clicking **Start**, selecting **All Programs, Accessories**, and then **Communications**, and then clicking **Remote Desktop Connection.**

Note: Windows 2000 does not include the Remote Desktop Connection application, however the application will run on Windows 2000. The application files can be copied from the Windows XP Embedded repositories on the development system to the remote computer running Windows 2000. To find the application files in the repositories:

a. *Open* **My Computer** *from the* **Start** *menu, and then browse to C:\Windows Embedded Data\Repositories.*

b. *From the* **View** *menu, select* **Explorer bar** *and then click on* **Search**.

c. *In the left pane, make sure that the search options are set to search sub-folders.*

d. *Type* **mstsc** *for the file name to search for, and then click the* **Search** *button.*

e. *From the search results, the files that are needed to run the Remote Desktop Connection application are* **mstsc.chm**, **mstsc.exe**, *and* **mstscax.dll**. *These files should be copied to the \Winnt\system32\ folder on the remote Windows 2000 system. They can be copied over the network, or copied onto a floppy disk and manually transferred.*

f. *The Remote Desktop Connection application can be run on the Windows 2000 system by selecting* **Run** *from the* **Start** *menu and typing* **mstsc.exe**.

2. Once the Remote Desktop Connection application is running on the remote computer, click the **Options** button to display the **Logon settings** in the **General** tab.

3. Type in the name of the XP Embedded target computer, **TARGET**, in the **Computer** field.

4. In the **User name** field, type **administrator**.

5. In the **Password** field, type the administrator password, **admin**.

6. Click the **Experience** tab and select the connection speed from the pull-down menu for your connection, such as **LAN (10 Mbps or higher)**.

7. There are several other options for the Remote Desktop Connection, which you are encouraged to view and modify as you wish. Once all of the desired settings have been configured, click the **Connect** button.

8. Once the connection has been successfully established, a window will appear displaying the desktop of the Windows XP Embedded target system. You can move the mouse cursor and operate the computer as if you were using a mouse and keyboard directly connected to the device.

Section 8.5 System Message Interception

There are two methods you can use for System Message Interception. The first method uses a native NTUSER feature, Enable Default Reply, to respond to a **MessageBox** function call with the default reply of the message box. For example, when a message box with an OK and Cancel button appears, you can have the system automatically select the default reply. If the default is OK, it will be the equivalent of clicking the OK button, but without any user interaction. Using this feature you may redirect the text message from a message box to an event log as well.

Another method to deal with system messages is to create a custom service, which will give you more control. Your Win32 custom service can scan the desktop and search for any window attribute, such as whether the window is visible, if it is a modal dialog window, and so on. You can get a lot more information by using a custom service than you can by using the default reply method. The Windows XP Embedded development kit CD includes a sample custom message interception program, *MessageBoxInstrument.c*, located in the folder \Samples\MBI\. More information on the API calls used to create a Win32 custom service can be found in the Windows Station and Desktop section and the Windows Reference section of the *Windows Platform SDK*.

In the next exercise, you will create and test a component which will enable the Default Reply feature and log messages to the Event Log.

Section 8.6 EXERCISE 11

Use Component Designer to create a new SLD file

1. Open **My Computer** from the **Start** menu.

2. Browse to the folder **C:\XPE dev** and create a new folder **C:\XPE dev\MBI SLD**.

3. Open **Component Designer** from the **Start** menu. Click **Start**, select **All Programs**, then **Windows Embedded Studio**, and click on **Component Designer**.

4. From the **File** menu, click **New**.

5. From the **File** menu, click **Save As**, browse to the folder **C:\XPE dev\MBI SLD** and save the file as **MessageBoxInterception.sld**.

6. Expand the **Windows XP Embedded Client** folder in the SLD Browser, right-click on **Components**, and then click on **Add Component**.

7. In the Details pane, type **Message Box Interception** in the **Name** property.

8. In the **Description** property of the Details pane, type:

```
Message Box Interception component uses the native NTUSER fea-
ture of Windows XP to enable default reply and event logging to
respond to MessageBox function calls.
```

Add registry data to the component

1. In the SLD Browser under the **Message Box Interception** component, right-click on **Registry Data**, select **Add**, and then click on **Registry Data**.

2. Click the **Browse** button to the right of the **Key name** property.

3. Browse to the registry path **HKEY_LOCAL_MACHINE\SYSTEM\CurrentControlSet\Control** and then click the **OK** button.

4. Append the string in the **Key name** property with the string **\Error Message Instrument**.

Note: Be sure to include the '\' character. The string in the Key name property should be HKEY_LOCAL_MACHINE\SYSTEM\CurrentControlSet\Control\Error Message Instrument.

5. Click the **Key only** property so that a green check appears in the checkbox.

6. Select the entire string in the **Key name** property, **SYSTEM\CurrentControlSet\Control\Error Message Instrument**, right-click on the selected text, and then click on **Copy**.

7. Click the **OK** button.

8. In the SLD Browser under the **Message Box Interception** component, right-click on **Registry Data**, select **Add**, and then click on **Registry Data**.

9. Right-click the mouse cursor inside the text box of the **Key name** property and click on **Paste**.

10. In the **Value name** property, type **EnableDefaultReply**.

11. Select **REG_DWORD** from the **Type** property pull-down menu.

12. In the **Value** property, type **1**.

13. Click the **OK** button.

14. Repeat the procedure from steps 8-13 to add the following registry values under the key **HKEY_LOCAL_MACHINE\SYSTEM\CurrentControlSet\Control\Error Message Instrument**:

Value name	Type	Value
EnableLogging	REG_DWORD	1
LogSeverity	REG_DWORD	0

Note: For this exercise, LogSeverity will have a value of 0. For future reference, LogSeverity can have any one of the values in the following table:

LogSeverity Data Value	Description
0x00000000 = EMI_SEVERITY_ALL	All message box events are logged.
0x00000001 = EMI_SEVERITY_USER	Message box events with the *dwStyle* parameter defined are logged, including MB_USERICON, MBICONASTERISK, MV_ICONQUESTION, MB_ICONEXCLAMATION, and MB_ICONHAND.
0x00000002 = EMI_SEVERITY_INFORMATI ON	Errors, warnings, questions, and information are logged. Message box events with no *dwStyle* parameter or *dwStyle* = MB_ICONUSER are not logged.
0x00000003 = EMI_SEVERITY_QUESTION	Errors, warnings, and questions are logged. Information, events with no style, and user-defined severity levels are not logged.
0x00000004 = EMI_SEVERITY_WARNING	Only errors and warnings are logged.
0x00000005 = EMI_SEVERITY_ERROR (EMI_SEVERITY_MAX_VALU E)	Only errors are logged.

Table 8.1 LogSeverity data values.

15. In the SLD Browser under the **Message Box Interception** component, right-click on **Registry Data**, select **Add**, and then click on **Registry Data**.

16. Click the **Browse** button to the right of the **Key name** property.

17. Browse to the registry path **HKEY_LOCAL_MACHINE\ SYSTEM\CurrentControlSet\Services\Eventlog\Application** and then click the **OK** button.

18. Append the string in the **Key name** property with the string **\Error Instrument**.

Note: Be sure to include the '\' character. The string in the Key name property should be HKEY_LOCAL_MACHINE\SYSTEM\CurrentControlSet\Services\Eventlog\Application\Error Instrument.

19. Click the **Key only** property so that a green check appears in the checkbox.

20. Select the entire string in the **Key name** property, **HKEY_LOCAL_MACHINE\ SYSTEM\CurrentControlSet\Services\Eventlog\Application\Error Instrument**, right-click on the selected text, and then click on **Copy**.

21. Click the **OK** button.

22. Using the same procedure in steps 8-13, add the following two registry values under the key **HKEY_LOCAL_MACHINE\ SYSTEM\CurrentControlSet\Services\Eventlog\Application\Error Instrument**

Value name	Type	Value
TypesSupported	REG_DWORD	7
EventMessageFile	REG_EXPAND_SZ	%SystemRoot%\System32\User32.dll

Add a component dependency

1. In the SLD browser under the **Message Box Interception** component, right-click on **Component or Group Dependency**, select **Add**, and then click on **Component Dependency**.

2. Since the system messages will be re-directed to the Event Log, you will create a dependency on the component that includes the Event Log tool so you can view the message in the event log. Click on the **Administration Support Tools** component, which is located under **Software : System : System Services : Base**, and then click the **OK** button.

Add shortcut resources

1. The shortcut resource will create a shortcut on the desktop for the eventvwr.exe application. In the SLD browser under the **Message Box Interception** component, right-click on **Resources**, select **Add**, and then click on **Shortcut**.

2. The Extended Properties can be modified individually by clicking on a property in the **Extended Properties** list and clicking on the **Edit** button. Make the following modifications to the Extended Properties listed below:

Extended Property Name	Change Value To:
DstName	Shortcut to Eventvwr.lnk
DstPath	%16409%
IconLocation	eventvwr.exe,0
TargetPath	%11%\ eventvwr.exe
WorkDir	%11%

3. Click the **OK** button.

Add group memberships to the component

1. In the SLD Browser under the **Message Box Interception** component, right-click on **Group Memberships** and select **Add Group Membership** to add the **Software : System : Management : Infrastructure** category group membership:

   a. Click the + on the left side of a node in the **Available groups** list to expand the node and view its child nodes. Expand the **Categories** root node, and then expand the **Software, System,** and **Management** nodes.

   b. Click the **Infrastructure** group and then click the **OK** button.

2. Right-click on **Group Memberships** and click on **Add Group Membership** to add the **Component Designer Exercises** package group membership:

   a. Click the + on the left side of a node in the **Available groups** list to expand the node and view its child nodes. Expand the **Packages** root node.

   a. Click the **Component Designer Exercises** group and then click the **OK** button.

3. Save the SLD file and close Component Designer.

Import the SLD file into the component database

1. Open Component Database Manager. Click on the **Start** menu, select **All Programs**, then select **Microsoft Windows Embedded Studio**, and click on **Component Database Manager**.

2. On the **Database** tab, click the **Import** button.

3. When the **Import SLD** window appears, click on the ellipsis [...] button to select the SLD file to import.

4. Browse to the folder **C:\XPE dev\MBI SLD**, select the file **MessageBox-Interception.sld**, and then click the **Open** button.

5. Click the **Import** button, and then click the **Close** button after the import process is complete.

6. You can verify that the component was imported into the database by clicking on the **Component** tab and locating the component in the list. The component can be more easily located by selecting the package **Component Designer Exercises** from the **Choose a package** pull-down menu. Click the **Close** button when finished.

Test the component in a run-time image

1. Open Target Designer. Click on the **Start** menu, select **All Programs**, then select **Microsoft Windows Embedded Studio**, and click on **Target Designer**.

2. Click **Open** on the **File** menu and browse to the folder **C:\XPE dev\TA_DATA**.

3. Assuming that you successfully completed the Target Designer exercise, select **TAPBASE.slx** and click the **Open** button.

4. From the **File** menu, select **Save As**.

5. In the **File name** text box, type **MBITest.slx** and then click the **Save** button.

6. In the Component Browser, add the **Message Box Interception** component from **Software : System : Management : Infrastructure**.

7. In the Configuration Editor, double-click the **User Interface Core** component to expand it, and then click on **Settings**.

8. In the Details Pane, click on the checkbox labeled **Show Desktop icons** so that a check appears.

9. Perform dependency check by selecting **Check Dependencies** from the **Configuration** menu.

10. Click the **Close** button when the dependency check is complete.

11. Build the run-time image by selecting **Build Target Image** from the **Configuration** menu.

12. If it is not already done, set the **Destination** folder as **C:\Windows Embedded Images**, then click the **Build** button. If prompted to perform a dependency check, click **No**. When prompted to delete the contents of the **Destination** folder, click **Yes**.

13. After the build process completes, click the **Close** button.

14. Save the configuration and close Target Designer.

15. Open **My Computer** from the **Start** menu and format the D: drive as **FAT**. WARNING! This will erase all data on D:!

16. Copy all of the *contents* of the folder **C:\Windows Embedded Images**, not the **Windows Embedded Images** folder itself, to **D:**.

17. Make sure that the boot.ini file is set up for a dual boot system. If this has not been done, refer to Exercise 6 of the Target Designer chapter.

18. Reboot the system into Windows XP Embedded.

19. After the FBA successfully completes, double-click on **Shortcut to Eventvwr** on the desktop to open the Event Viewer.

20. Right-click on **System**, and then click on **Clear all Events**. A **Save File** window should appear; click the **Cancel** button. Normally, Event Viewer displays a message box asking if you would like to save the events to a file before clearing the events. With **Default reply** enabled, the message box was intercepted. The default reply of the message box that prompts to save the events to a file is **Yes**, and that is why the **Save File** window appears immediately.

21. The message displayed by the message box was recorded in the event log. Click **Application** and then double-click on the most recent event recorded. The events in the event log whose **Source** is **Error Instrument** are actually the messages from message boxes that are intercepted into the event log.

Section 8.7 Enhanced Write Filter

The Windows XP Embedded operating system is capable of booting from read-only media, such as a CD-ROM, flash ROM, or a protected hard drive. It is the **Enhanced Write Filter (EWF)** that enables the operating system to boot from read-only media. EWF also maintains the appearance of read/write access to the operating system. Using EWF, the contents of a volume on the target media are protected by redirecting all writes to an alternative storage location called an overlay. In this context, an overlay is similar to a transparency overlay on an overhead projector. Any change made to the top overlay affects the image as it is seen projected on the screen, but if the top overlay is removed, the underlying picture remains unchanged.

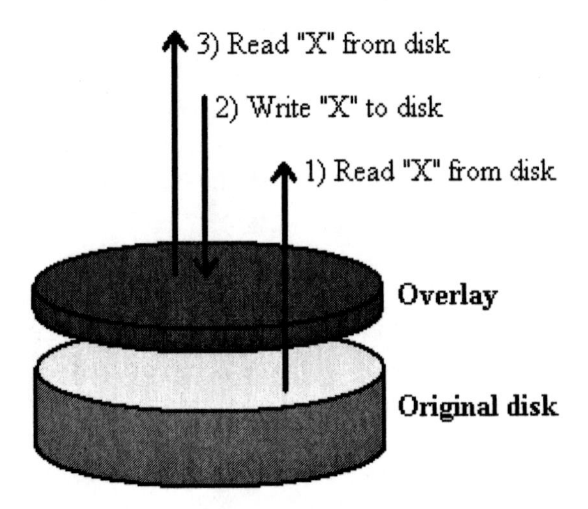

Figure 8.1 Using the Enhanced Write Filter, the overlay layer prevents the original data on the disk from being overwritten.

Section 8.7.1 Overlay Types

For each protected volume you can select from one of two types of overlays to retain the overlay information: RAM and Disk. A **RAM overlay** uses system memory to store overlay data; writes to the disk are re-directed to system memory. When using a RAM overlay, Windows XP Embedded does not require persistent read/write storage to run. However, all overlay data is lost when the system is shut down or rebooted.

With a **Disk overlay**, the information is retained after rebooting. Disk overlays use a pre-designated disk partition called the EWF Volume to retain overlay information. All writes to the disk are re-directed to the EWF Volume. When using a Disk overlay, the EWF allows you to layer more than one overlay on top of a protected volume. Therefore you can peel overlay layers off the top of the overlay stack to restore the view of the volume back to a prior state. Up to 9 overlay layers, also called overlay levels, can be used.

Section 8.7.2 EWF Volume

The EWF Volume is created and formatted at the first boot of a run-time image. It is created from unallocated space on the disk and is not visible or recognized by the operating system. When the FBA completes processing, any error creating or formatting the EWF volume will be logged to the FBALOG.txt file in the \Windows\FBA\ folder. The EWF Volume stores the EWF master volume table, overlay stack, and overlay data. The EWF master volume table stores information about the EWF Volume. Each overlay stack corresponds to a protected volume and is partitioned into multiple levels that correspond to a checkpoint. There can be only one EWF Volume, but there can be more than one protected volume (up to 9). It is possible to have some volumes protected by Disk overlays with others protected by RAM overlays.

The Enhanced Write Filter does not protect dynamic disks. All protected volumes must be configured as basic disks. EWF does not process disk writes to removable read/write media, such as a floppy disk or Zip drive, or external drives, such as a USB/1394 HDD or CD.

Section 8.7.3 EWF Components and Files

There are three components involved in using the Enhanced Write Filter feature: the EWF NTLDR, EWF Manager Console application, and Enhanced Write Filter components.

The **EWF NTLDR** component is needed only when the Enhanced Write Filter uses a Disk overlay, when booting from writable media. It includes a modified version of NT Loader which understands the overlay mapping structure of the EWF Volume. EWF NTLDR is able to load the most recent image of the operating system and access any changes that were made to the system prior to the last boot of the system.

Including the **EWF Manager Console application** component enables you to use the Ewfmgr.exe application. With the Ewfmgr.exe application, you can report the status of each protected volume overlay, report the format of the overall EWF configurations, and issue a set of commands to the Enhanced Write Filter driver, including the ability to peel overlay levels from a disk overlay. To list the command line options and their function, type **ewfmgr.exe /?**.

The **Enhanced Write Filter** component is the main component of the feature. It includes the files that make up the feature. **Ewf.sys** is the filter driver responsible for redirecting disk-write I/O Request Packets (IRPs) to the EWF overlay so that the original disk is unchanged. For read-only IRPs, the filter driver searches for a matching disk sector in the current overlay stack. If it is found, the sector is retrieved from the overlay stack, otherwise it is retrieved from the original disk. The filter driver includes an INF file, **Ewf.inf**, whose only purpose is to identify the enhanced write filter to the system so that it does not show up as an "unknown" device. **Ewfdll.dll** creates the EWF Volume and configures the enhanced write filter during FBA execution. **Ewfinit.dll** is invoked by the First Boot Agent and is responsible for formatting the EWF Volume.

Section 8.7.4 Enhanced Write Filter Settings

The Enhanced Write Filter component has settings that can be divided into two groups. One group of settings is global for the Enhanced Write Filter as it relates to the run-time image. The global settings specify the number of protected volumes, the maximum number of overlay levels, and the EWF volume size. EWF can protect up to 9 volumes and each volume can have up to 9 overlay levels. Once these two properties have been set in Target Designer, they cannot be changed. When using disk overlays, the EWF partition size should be large enough to accommodate the total size of all the volumes being protected by a disk overlay EWF. Only one EWF volume can exist on the system and you should leave enough unallocated space on the disk for the EWF volume; enough space to accommodate at least the size specified in the EWF partition size property. Once the EWF volume becomes full, it exhibits the same behavior as any volume that becomes full. You can either delete files to free space or peel off overlay levels.

EWF Volume Configuration	
Maximum Number of Protected Volumes	1
Maximum Number of Overlay Levels	1
EWF Partition Size in KBytes	0

Protected Volume # 1	
Start EWF Enabled	☑
Enable Lazy Write	☐
Disk Number	0
Partition Number	1
Disk Type	IDE
Overlay Type	RAM
Optimization Option	◉ Optimal Performance ○ Use Less Overlay Space ○ Use Less Overlay Space & Less Writes
Previous Volume	Next Volume

Figure 8.2 Enhanced Write Filter settings.

The other group of settings is specific to each protected volume. When more than one volume is being protected, the **Next Volume** and **Previous Volume** buttons are used to step through each protected volume's settings page. The available settings for each protected volume are described below:

- **Start EWF Enabled** – When checked, as it is by default, the property specifies that EWF will start protecting the disk immediately after first boot.

- **Enable Lazy Write** – When checked, the protected volume mapping data is written to cache to improve performance. EWF flushes the cache to disk in an optimized way, usually as a background activity. Basically, it reduces writes to the EWF volume, which can help extend the life of flash media.

- **Disk Number** – Specifies the disk number of the protected volume. Disk numbers are zero-based, which means that the first disk is disk number 0.
- **Partition Number** – Specifies the partition number of the protected volume. Partition numbers are one-based, which means that the first partition on the disk is partition number 1.
- **Disk Type** – Specifies whether the disk is IDE or SCSI.
- **Overlay Type** – Specifies whether the overlay data will be written to a Disk overlay or a RAM overlay.
- **Optimization Option** – An option can be selected to determine how EWF handles its own internal allocation within the EWF partition in order to achieve the goal of optimized speed, space, or write frequency to disk. The following options are available:

  a. Optimal Performance (default setting): Provides the fastest execution, but uses more EWF partition space.

  b. Use Less Overlay Space: Consumes less EWF partition space, but is slower than the Optimal Performance option. When EWF needs to allocate a new sector inside the EWF partition, it performs a comparison between the new data and existing data on the disk. If the data is the same, allocation will be skipped.

  c. Use Less Overlay Space & Less Writes: Regardless of whether there is an allocation or not, a comparison is performed between the new data and existing data on the disk when EWF needs to write to a sector inside the EWF partition. Of the three available optimization options, this is the slowest, but it uses the least amount of writes, which is useful in extending the life of the persistent storage device if it is a flash device.

In the next exercise, you will create a run-time image which uses the Enhanced Write Filter. Steps will be taken to reduce the size of the footprint, including using the results from TA.exe to create a configuration. The exercise assumes that the Target Analyzer and Target Designer exercises in Chapters 5 and 6 have been completed.

Section 8.8 EXERCISE 12

Create a new Target Designer configuration and import the results of TA.exe

1. Launch Target Designer. From the **Start** menu, select **All Programs**, select **Windows Embedded Studio**, and click on **Target Designer**.

Note: If you already created a TA.exe-based configuration in the Target Designer chapter exercise, where you imported the results of TA.exe and immediately saved a post import copy of the configuration (TAPostImport.slx), which was recommended, you can skip step 2 and steps 5 through 11 to save some time. Instead of performing those steps, all you need to do is make a copy of the file TAPostImport.slx, rename the copy EWFDemo.slx, and open EWFDemo.slx in Target Designer. Otherwise, proceed with Step 2 below.

2. From the **File** menu, select **New**. Name the configuration **EWFDemo**.

3. In the Configuration Editor, expand the configuration root, **EWFDemo.slx**, and click on **Settings**. If **Settings** is the only resource displayed under the configuration root node and you wish to view the other resources in the configuration editor, select **Resources** from the **View** menu.

4. In the Details Pane under **Available Settings**, click the **Target Device Settings** link, and then click on the **show** link. Since the image is to be deployed to the hard drive's second partition (the D: drive), the settings should be set as in the figure below.

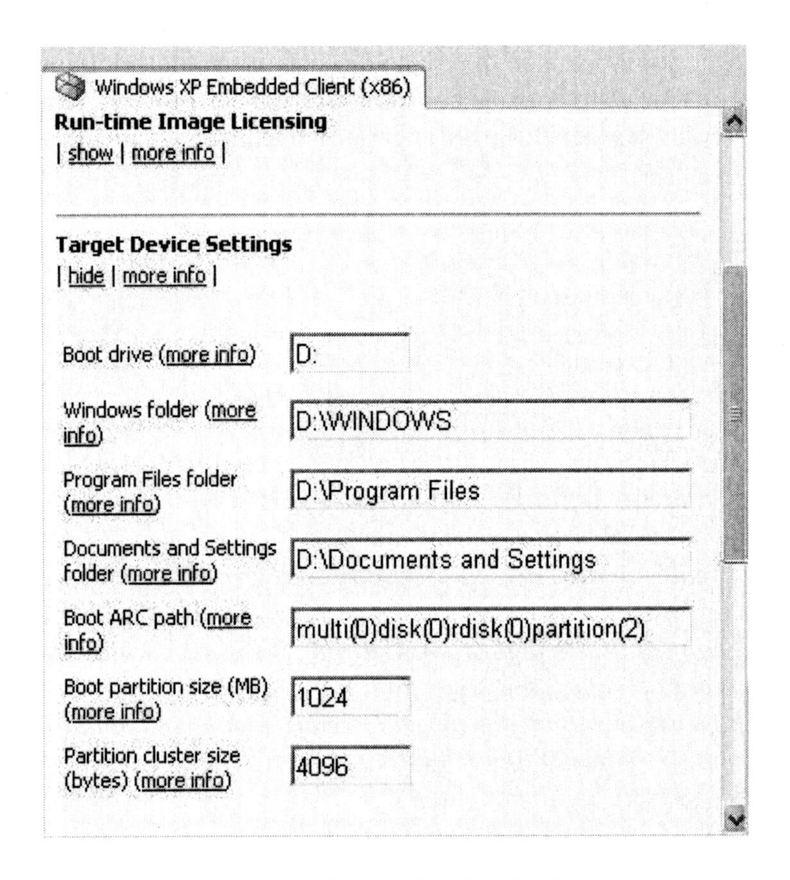

Figure 8.3 Target Device Settings

5. From the **File** menu, select **Import**, browse to the folder **C:\XPE dev\TA_DATA**, and then select the file **dev_ta.pmq**. This assumes that the Target Analyzer Exercise 5 has been completed. If not, return to Exercise 5 in Chapter 5 and follow the instructions to create a Target Analyzer output file.

6. On the **Import File** dialog, copy just the path, **C:\XPE dev\TA_DATA**, from the **File** text box to the **Log File** text box. Append the path with the log file name **ta_import.log**. The string in the **Log File** property should read **C:\XPE dev\TA_DATA\ta_import.log**.

7. Click the **Start** button. The import process may take several minutes.

8. Once the PMQ import is complete, click the **Close** button to close the **Import File** dialog.

9. From the **File** menu, select **Save As**, and then browse to the folder **C:\ XPE dev\TA_DATA**. Make sure that the name of the file is **EWFDemo.slx**, then click the **Save** button.

Note: The optional steps below are for saving the configuration while it is in a particular state, which was recommended in the Target Designer chapter. It is a good practice in case a mistake was made and the configuration needs to be returned to a previous state.

10. (Optional) To save a copy of the TA.exe-based configuration in the post import state, select **Save As** from the **File** menu. Right-click on the file **EWFDemo.slx** and select **Copy**. On the keyboard, press the Ctrl key and the 'v' key at the same time.

11. (Optional) Right-click on the file **Copy of EWFDemo.slx** and select **Rename**. Rename the copied file **TAPostImport.slx**, and then click the **Cancel** button.

Remove unwanted components to reduce the image size

1. If they exist, remove the **Advanced Configuration and Power Interface (ACPI) PC** and the **Microsoft ACPI-Compliant System** components from the configuration editor.

2. Remove any other ACPI device components from the configuration editor.

3. To replace the ACPI Computer, add the **Standard PC** component, which is located in the Component Browser under the category **Hardware : Devices : Computers**.

4. Expand the **Standard PC** component in the configuration editor and click on **Settings**.

5. In the details pane, click the **show** link under **System Identification** and type **TARGET** in the **Computer name** field.

6. If any components related to the following types of devices exist in the configuration, remove them:

- Serial Ports / Parallel Ports / Communication Ports / Printer Port
- Audio Devices / Game Ports
- USB Devices
- Monitor Devices

Note: Typically, the name of the component will describe the type of device that the component is for. For example, it can safely be assumed that any component which has the substring "USB" in the component name is a component for a USB device. Therefore, every component in the configuration whose name includes the substring "USB" can be removed for this exercise. Some components that you attempt to remove might be added back in after a dependency check. It only means that you tried to remove a component that is required by some other component or components.

7. Add the components in the following table in order to satisfy the minimum requirements to have a working run-time image:

Component	Location
Default Monitor	Hardware : Devices : Monitors
Disk drive*	Hardware : Devices : Disk drives
Logical disk manager	Hardware : Devices : System devices
Plug and Play Software Device Enumerator	Hardware : Devices : System devices
Primary IDE channel	Hardware : Devices : IDE ATA/ATAPI controllers
Secondary IDE channel	Hardware : Devices : IDE ATA/ATAPI controllers

*There are three components in the Component Browser named "Disk drive". A way to distinguish between them is to add all three and view their resources. If you are unsure of which one will work for you, it will do no harm to leave all three in there.

8. From the **File** menu, click **Save**.

9. (Optional) To save a copy of the minimized configuration, select **Save As** from the **File** menu. Right-click on the file **EWFDemo.slx** and select **Copy**. On the keyboard, press the Ctrl key and the 'v' key at the same time.

10. (Optional) Right-click on the file **Copy of EWFDemo.slx** and select **Rename**. Rename the copied file **TAMinRequirements.slx**, and then click the **Cancel** button.

Include and configure additional components for this exercise

1. Add the following components for the Enhanced Write Filter feature:

Component	Location
Enhanced Write Filter	Software : System : System Services : Base
EWF NTLDR	Software : System : System Services : Base
EWF Manager Console application	Software : Applications : Management

2. Configure the Enhanced Write Filter. In the configuration editor, double-click on the **Enhanced Write Filter** component and select **Settings.**

3. Configure the **EWF Volume Configuration** settings as follows:

   a. Maximum Number of Protected Volumes: 2

   b. Maximum Number of Overlay Levels: 1

   c. EWF Partition Size in Kbytes: 34816

Note: Normally you would want the EWF Partition Size to be large enough to accommodate all of the protected volumes, but you won't be doing much with it in this exercise so 34MB will be sufficient.

4. Configure the **Protected Volume #1** settings as follows:

   a. Start EWF Enabled – Checked

   b. Enable Lazy Write – Unchecked

   c. Disk Number: 0

   d. Partition Number: 1

   e. Disk Type: IDE

   f. Overlay Type: DISK

   g. Optimization Options: Optimal Performance

5. Click the **Next Volume** button and then configure the **Protected Volume #2** settings as follows:

   a. Start EWF Enabled – Checked

   b. Enable Lazy Write – Unchecked

   c. Disk Number: 0

   d. Partition Number: 2

   e. Disk Type: IDE

   f. Overlay Type: RAM

   g. Optimization Options: Optimal Performance

6. Add the **Misc. Command Line Tools** component, which is located in the SLD Browser under the category **Software : System : System Services : Base**.

7. Add the **Task Manager** component, which is located in the SLD Browser under the category **Software : System : User Interface : Shells : Windows Shell**.

8. Perform a dependency check by clicking **Dependency Check** from the **Configuration** menu.

9. Resolve all the dependency errors in the **Task** list and then perform another dependency check. Repeat the process until the dependency check completes without errors. Use the table below as a guide to resolve the dependency errors:

Task	System Requirement	Resolution
Component: "Regional and Language Options […]"	Language support.	Add the "English Language Support" component.
Component: "Session Manager (Windows subsystem) […]"configuration.	Login process.	Add the "MinLogon" component.
Component: "Standard PC […]"	File system.	Add both "FAT" and "NTFS" components.
Component: "MinLogon […]"	Shell.	Add the "Command shell" component.

Table 8.2 Dependency Error Resolution

Build and deploy the run-time image

1. To build the image, click **Build Target Image** from the **Configuration** menu.

2. Make sure that the **Build type** is **Release**, the **Destination** is **C:\Windows Embedded Images**, and the **Log file** is **C:\XPE dev\TA_DATA\EWF-Demo.log**, and then click the **Build** button.

3. When prompted to run a dependency check, you can click the **No** button if you are sure that your last dependency check finished with no errors.

4. When prompted to delete all contents of the destination folder, click the **Yes** button.

5. After the build process has successfully completed, click the **Close** button.

6. Save the configuration and close Target Designer.

7. Open **My Computer** from the **Start** menu and format the D: drive as **FAT**. WARNING! This will erase all data on D:!

8. Copy all the *contents* of the folder **C:\Windows Embedded Images**, not the **Windows Embedded Images** folder itself, to **D:**.

9. Make sure that the boot.ini file is set up for a dual boot system. If this has not been done, refer to Exercise 6 of the Target Designer chapter.

10. Reboot the system to Windows XP Embedded and allow the First Boot Agent to run.

Test the Enhanced Write Filter

1. To view information about the Enhanced Write Filter, type **ewfmgr**. If there was an error in creating the EWF Volume, check the FBALOG.txt file in the **\Windows\FBA** folder.

2. Typing **ewfmgr -?** lists all of the ewfmgr commands.

3. To view information about one of the protected volumes, type **ewfmgr c:** or **ewfmgr d:**. To view information about all protected volumes, type **ewfmgr -all**. Take note of the **Disk Space Used**. The operating system uses 32 kilo-bytes for boot information.

4. At the command prompt, type **copy d:\ntldr d:\ntldr2**.

5. Now type **ewfmgr d:**. You should notice a change in the **Disk Space Used**.

6. To shut down the Windows XP Embedded system, type **shutdown –l** at the command prompt.

Section 8.9 Flash Media

There are some advantages to using flash semiconductor memory. The physical dimensions are typically smaller and power consumption is typically lower than mechanical drives. Many embedded systems use flash memory for this reason, and to eliminate potential problems that may be caused by environmental factors, such as shock and vibration. Because it is not mechanical, read access time is significantly faster on a flash device than on a hard disk. Windows XP Embedded supports booting and running from flash media.

Typically, writing to a flash device is a two-step process. A cell is first erased, then is written to. You may need a custom file system implementation to handle this process if you want the flash device to behave as a typical writeable storage device.

Devices such as CompactFlash, FlashDrive, Type I and II PCMCIA cards, MMCs and Memory Stick will be supported by Windows XP Embedded as long as the device emulates a disk via SCSI or IDE interface through an ATA or SCSI driver. For devices that do not emulate an ATA device, there are existing Windows XP components that contain the appropriate Windows driver for the device. You can view a list of the available components under the category Hardware : Devices : PCMCIA and Flash memory devices.

Section 8.10 El Torito Bootable CD-ROM

Windows XP Embedded comes with tools and components which enable you to create a run-time image that will boot and run from CD-ROM. The build must include the Enhanced Write Filter feature and the El Torito CD component. The El Torito CD component implements the El Torito specification, which provides a standard for creating a bootable CD-ROM. The El Torito specification allows for the creation of a CD-ROM as the image of a hard disk drive. When you create an image of a hard disk, the CD-ROM will boot as drive C: and all hard drive letters will be shifted up one letter. Further information about the El Torito specification can be found at http://www.phoenix.com/resources/specs-cdrom.pdf.

Included in the Windows Embedded Studio suite is the El Torito CD image preparation tool, Hd2iso.exe, which is located in the folder \Program Files\Windows Embedded\Utilities. This tool converts one or more hard disk partitions to an ISO 9660/El Torito-compliant image file that can be burned to a CD using a commercial CD-burning application. ISO 9660 is a file system for CD-ROM. Up to four partitions can be selected to make up the ISO 9660 image, but the total combined size of the included partitions cannot exceed the size of the CD on which the image will be burned. Available CD sizes are 74 minute (650 megabyte) and 80 minute (700 megabyte).

The basic steps involved in creating a Windows XP Embedded El Torito system are:

1. Build an El Torito run-time image.
2. Transfer the image to a FAT boot partition.
3. Convert the pre-FBA run-time image partition to an ISO image and burn it to a CD.
4. Insert the ISO image CD into the drive, but boot from the hard disk that contains the image to allow the FBA to run.
5. Run the etprep.exe tool.
6. Convert the post-FBA run-time image to an ISO image and burn it to a CD.
7. Boot the run-time image from the El Torito CD.

Within these steps there are many small details that can cause problems if not attended to. The next exercise steps you through the complex process of creating a bootable CD. Because of the complexity of the process, the exercise will contain more detail between some of the steps to help explain the process and options for creating the bootable CD. Unlike previous exercises in this book, you will learn the details of the topic while you are performing the exercise rather than beforehand.

Also, this exercise has the following additional requirements for the system:

- An additional, clean hard drive. It should be large enough to store up to 650 or 700 megabytes of data.
- A BIOS that supports booting from CD-ROM.
- At least one CD-ROM drive.
- A CD-burner and a CD authoring application that enables you to create an ISO-9660 CD from an ISO-9660 image file.
- 2 blank CDs.

Section 8.11 EXERCISE 13

Connect the target media and partition the disk

Note: The "Windows method" of preparing the target media, which was described in the Build Overview chapter, is being used in this exercise. If you are using a separate machine as a target device, the alternative "DOS method" might be more convenient for you. The drawback of the DOS method is that it requires the purchase of a third party tool to connect to the target media, such as Remote Recover, and you must create a DOS boot floppy that contains the fdisk and format disk utilities, which requires you to have DOS. The Windows method uses the disk tools of the development operating system and does not require the additional purchase of Remote Recover or MSDOS. All that matters is that there is some way for the development operating system to connect to the target media so that the XP Embedded run-time image can be copied to it.

1. Connect the additional target hard disk to the development machine. The setup may vary from one computer to another. For example, if you connect your target hard disk on the same IDE cable that your development hard disk is on, you will have to set the target disk's jumper setting to configure the disk as a slave device. You might have to get into the BIOS settings to get the BIOS to recognize the newly added target hard disk. The development OS will need to access the target disk.

2. Boot the machine to the development OS (Windows 2000 or Windows XP Professional).

3. Launch the disk manager by right-clicking **My Computer** on the **Start** menu and clicking on **Manage**.

4. In the left pane, expand the **Computer Management (local)** node, expand the **Storage** node, and then select **Disk Management**.

5. In the lower right window, you should see the target disk. If there are any partitions on it, delete them by right-clicking the partition, selecting **Delete Partition**, and clicking the **Yes** button on the deletion confirmation pop-up window.

6. Create a new partition on the target disk by right-clicking in the **Unallocated** space of the target hard disk and selecting **New Partition** from the menu.

Note: You are creating a partition that will be used to boot the run-time image for the first time in order for FBA to run. Also, the Hd2iso tool will create an ISO image file based on the partitions that exist on this disk. If, for example, you wanted your ISO 9660 CD to have a C: partition and a D: partition, you would create two partitions on the hard drive and indicate the two partitions in the Hd2iso tool. The total combined size of the partitions must be less than the capac-

ity of the CD. Also, you must leave at least at least 4 KB of unallocated space on the target hard disk so that an EWF configuration partition can be placed there during the FBA.

7. When the **New Partition Wizard** appears, click the **Next** button.

8. Make sure that **Primary partition** is selected on the screen that follows and then click the **Next** button.

9. For the **Partition size in MB**, type in **600** and then click the **Next** button.

Note: For this exercise, you will create one 600 megabyte partition, which should be more than enough space to store the XP Embedded image that will eventually be burned on CD.

10. This screen prompts you to assign a drive letter to the partition, which will be used by the development operating system to identify and access the disk. The drive letter that is assigned in the development OS will have no effect on the XP Embedded image that exists on the disk, so the default selection on this screen should be sufficient. Take note of the drive letter assigned to the target disk and then click the **Next** button to continue.

11. Make sure that **Format this partition with the following settings** is selected and set the following settings:

    a. **File System** – **FAT**

    b. **Allocation unit size – Default**

    c. **Volume label** – (This doesn't really matter; leave it blank if you wish).

    d. **Perform a quick format** – checked.

12. Click the **Next** button.

13. Click the **Finish** button to complete the New Partition Wizard.

14. Right-click on the new partition that you just created on the target disk and select **Mark Partition as Active**.

15. Close the **Computer Management** console.

Build an El Torito run-time image

Note: Since you have already built some run-time images in previous exercises, you can use one of those configurations as a starting point for building your El Torito image. For example, you can use the TAPBASE.slx configuration and add the functionality to make it an El Torito image. It is recommended that you make a copy of the configuration file that you wish to use so that the original configuration will remain intact.

1. Open Target Designer. Click on the **Start** menu, select **All Programs**, then select **Microsoft Windows Embedded Studio**, and click on **Target Designer**.

2. Click **Open** on the **File** menu and browse to the folder **C:\XPE dev\TA_DATA**.

3. Assuming that you successfully completed the Target Designer exercise, select **TAPBASE.slx** and click the **Open** button.

4. From the **File** menu, select **Save As**.

5. In the **File name** text box, type **CDImage.slx** and then click the **Save** button.

6. In the Configuration Editor, expand the root node, **CDImage.slx**, and click **Settings**.

7. In the Details pane, click the **Target Device Settings** link, and then click the **show** link under **Target Device Settings**.

8. The Target Device Settings should be as follows:

    a. **Boot drive**: **C:**

    b. **Windows folder**: **C:\WINDOWS**

    c. **Program Files folder**: **C:\Program Files**

    d. **Documents and Settings folder**: **C:\Documents and Settings**

    e. **Boot ARC path**: **multi(0)disk(0)rdisk(0)partition(1)**

Note: The C: drive and partition 1 are being specified because when the run-time image is ready to be booted for the first time on the hard drive, you will disconnect the hard drive that contains the development OS and set the jumper settings of the target hard disk as Master. Also, when you burn the final image on the CD, that CD will boot as the C: drive.

9. In the configuration editor, delete the **NT Loader, NTFS, NTFS Format,** and **Primitive: Untfs** components from the configuration.

*Note: The **FAT Format** and **FAT** file system components need to be included in the configuration. The directions in previous exercises that created configurations specified this, so if you are using a previous configuration, it should already be there. If not, the **FAT Format** component can be added from the SLD browser category **Software : System : Storage & File Systems : Applications**, and the **FAT** component can be added from the SLD category **Software : System : Storage & File Systems : Infrastructure : File Systems**.*

10. From the SLD browser, add the **EWF Manager Console application** component, which is located under the category **Software : Applications : Management**.

11. From the SLD browser, add the **El Torito CD, EWF NTLDR**, and **Enhanced Write Filter** components. All three of these components are located under the category **Software : System : System Services : Base**.

12. To configure the Enhanced Write Filter, expand the **Enhanced Write Filter** component in the Configuration Editor and click **Settings**. After adding the **Enhanced Write Filter** component, the only setting you will need to change is to uncheck the **Start EWF Enabled** setting. The **Enhanced Write Filter** settings should be as follows:

    a. **Maximum Number of Protected Volumes**: **1**

    b. **Maximum Number of Overlay Levels**: **1**

    c. **EWF Partition Size in Kbytes**: **0**

    d. **Start EWF Enabled – Unchecked**

    e. **Enable Lazy Write – Unchecked**

    f. **Disk Number**: **0**

    g. **Partition Number**: **1**

    h. **Disk Type**: **IDE**

    i. **Overlay Type**: **RAM**

    j. **Optimization Options**: **Optimal Performance**

*Note: The **El Torito CD** component has a setting for you to change the disk signature if you wish. It is a number displayed in decimal. The default is 1330924613, which is 0x4F544C45 in hexadecimal. Therefore, the disk signature is "ELTO": 0x45, 0x4c, 0x54, 0x4f. If you change this setting in Target Designer, you have to enter the same number in the Hd2iso tool (except it will be in hexadecimal form). Leaving it at the default value will work fine. The only reason you would have to change this setting is if you planned to have another disk on the system that has the same disk signature.*

13. In the Configuration Editor, double-click the **User Interface Core** component to expand it, and then click on **Settings**.

14. In the Details Pane, click on the checkbox labeled **Show Run on Start Menu** so that a check appears.

12. Make sure that the **Auto-resolve dependencies** feature is enabled and then perform a dependency check by selecting **Check Dependencies** from the **Configuration** menu. Click the **Close** button when the dependency check is complete.
15. Resolve any dependency errors if there are any. After each set of dependency errors has been resolved, continue running dependency checks until a dependency check completes with no errors.

Note: Since this configuration is based on the TAPBASE configuration and the auto-resolve dependencies feature is enabled, there probably won't be any dependency errors that require user interaction.

16. Build the run-time image by clicking **Build Target Image** from the **Configuration** menu. Click the **Close** button after the build process successfully completes.

17. Save the configuration and close Target Designer.

18. Open **My Computer** from the **Start** menu, if it isn't already open, and copy all the contents of the build destination folder (which is C:\Windows Embedded Images by default) but not the folder itself, onto the target hard drive partition.

Create an ISO 9660 image CD using Hd2iso.exe

Note: The system will not boot from this CD. In fact, this disk will eventually be discarded. The reason for creating the disk is so that the eltorito.sys driver can detect and enumerate the volume for the first time. This allows a full disk stack to be installed on top of the device, the volume to be mounted and assigned a drive letter, and all pertinent data to be stored in the registry during the First Boot Agent execution.

1. Open a command window by selecting **Run** from the **Start** menu and typing **cmd**.

2. Type **cd \Program Files\Windows Embedded\Utilities** and press the **Enter** key.

3. Launch the Hd2iso tool by typing **hd2iso**.

4. From the **Main Menu**, select option **1. Create an ISO-9660/ELTORITO bootable image file.**

5. From the **Iso Image Menu**, select **2. Set physical drive.**

6. Select your target hard drive from the **Set Physical Drive** menu. If you connected your target hard drive as a primary slave, you would select **1. \\.\PhysicalDrive1.**

7. From the **Iso Image Menu**, select **3. Select partition(s).**

8. From the **Select Partitions** menu, select the number that corresponds to the partition that you created on your target hard disk. If there are any more partitions that you would like to include in your ISO image, you can select the number that corresponds to each partition. You can only select partitions that are on the same disk. The total size of the selected partitions cannot exceed the capacity of the CD that you will burn the ISO image on. Press the **P** key when you are done selecting partitions to include in your ISO image.

9. From the **Iso Image Menu**, select **4. Set image file path.**

10. Type the full path and file name of the ISO image file, **C:\osboot.iso**. This is the resulting file produced by the hd2iso tool that will be used to create the bootable CD. The file will be as large as the total size of the partitions you selected in Step 8 of this exercise.

11. From the **Iso Image Menu**, select **5. Advanced Options.**

Note: You may not need to configure any of the Advanced Options. Below is a description of each option:

- **Select target media size** enables you to select the size of the CD that the ISO image is to be deployed to, either a 74-minute (650 MB) or an 80-minute (700 MB) disk.

- **Specify disk signature** allows you to change the disk signature here, but it must match the disk signature that was built in your run-time image in the El Torito CD component settings. By default, these settings match in the hd2iso tool and the El Torito CD component settings in Target Designer, so there should be no need to change them.

- **Specify volume ID** enables you to label the volume. The volume label will appear in My Computer next to the CD drive, but this property has no effect on functionality.

- **Specify a binary file for inclusion in the System Data Area** enables you to specify a binary file whose contents will be copied into the System Data Area of the image. The type of data or use for this data is not defined, but engineers typically use it to store proprietary information for their specific BIOSs, such as security checksums.

- **Select partition to boot** enables you to specify one of your other selected partitions to boot from instead of the first partition. It marks the partition as bootable. You must specify the first partition on the image to maintain functionality, but you can override that flag with this option. If the partition you wish to boot from is already marked bootable, you don't need to change anything here.

12. When you are done configuring the **Advanced Options**, press **P** to return to the **Iso Image Menu**.

13. From the **Iso Image Menu**, select **6. Create image** to create the ISO 9660 image.

14. After the image has been created, press any key to return to the **Iso Image Menu**, and then press the **Q** key to exit the Hd2iso tool. To close the command window, type **exit**.

15. Burn the ISO 9660 image onto a CD. Select the file **C:\osboot.iso**. Your CD authoring application needs to support the ability to read an ISO image file and create an ISO CD from the contents of the image file. Usually CD burning software has a flag in the options or will prompt you to ask if you would like to create a disk with the contents of the ISO file. Adaptec EZ-CD Pro is an example of a CD authoring package that can create an ISO disk.

Boot the system from the target hard disk so the FBA can run

1. After the pre-FBA ISO CD has been created, insert it into the CD drive that will be used to boot the ISO CD.

2. Shut down the system and unplug the power cord.

3. Remove the hard disk that contains the development OS and tools.

4. Set the jumper of the target hard disk to be configured as Master.

5. Plug the power cord back in and power up the system.

6. Get into the BIOS settings and make sure that the system will attempt to boot from the hard disk before trying to boot from CD.

7. Exit the BIOS settings and allow Windows XP Embedded to boot from the hard disk.

8. Verify that the Enhanced Write Filter was properly configured by using the EWF Manager console application; type **ewfmgr c:**. After the First Boot Agent has successfully completed, open a command window by selecting **Run** from the **Start** menu and typing **cmd**.

9. At this point you can change any settings that you would like on your final CD, such as changing the desktop background if you have the Display Control Panel built into your image. You can also modify the boot.ini file to set up the system for dual booting if you plan to have a hard disk connected to the machine that will run the El Torito CD.

10. When you are ready to finalize your run-time image, run the El Torito preparation utility. In the command window, type **etprep -all**. The system must be immediately shut down after running etprep.exe. The embedded partition will no longer boot after etprep.exe is run.

Note: The etprep utility serves two purposes:

- Deletes the EWF configuration partition. This will cause the EWF to enable itself at the next boot. When EWF loads and finds that it has no configuration partition, it will look in the registry under HKEY_LOCAL_MACHINE\System\CurrentControlSet\Services\EWF\Parameters to determine which volume it is to protect.

- Swaps the drive letters of the El Torito disk device and the original source partition so that the El Torito CD appears as the C: drive.

11. After the system has been shut down, unplug the power cord, configure the jumper on the target hard disk as a slave device, reconnect the development disk, and boot into the development OS.

12. Repeat the procedure in the previous section (***Create an ISO 9660 image CD using Hd2iso.exe***) to create a final version of your El Torito CD. You will need another blank CD.

13. To test the El Torito CD, reboot the system with the CD in the drive. You will have to get into the BIOS settings and set the boot order so that the system will boot from the CD drive first.

This chapter introduced you to the Windows XP Embedded Enabling features. The basic features were described in detail, with particular attention paid to shell customization, headless operation, remote management, system message interception, the enhanced write filter, and booting and running from flash media and CD-ROM. It was also discussed how some of the features interact with each other, such as system message interception with headless operation and the enhanced write filter with a bootable CD-ROM. Embedded enabling features were then utilized in exercises for remote management, system message interception, the enhanced write filter, and the bootable CD-ROM feature. The next chapter will cover some advanced component authoring techniques, which will be used to create a custom shell component.

CHAPTER 9 Advanced Component Authoring Techniques

Creating a component can be quite a challenge in some cases, especially for a component that encompasses third party software, such as an application or device driver. You may not know exactly how the software interacts with the registry and file system, and thus you may not know which files and registry data to include in the component. Fortunately, there are helpful tools available, in Windows Embedded Studio and from third parties, which will assist in gathering information about a binary file.

Section 9.1 Component Conversion

Components do not always need to be created from scratch. Windows XP Embedded includes tools that can convert INF and PMQ files into component definition (SLD) files. There are two methods to convert these types of files into a component. The first method is to import the PMQ or INF file into Component Designer. The second method is to use the command line tool Econvert.exe. One of the main differences between the two methods is how the tool handles a file reference when an INF file is imported. In Component Designer, if the INF importer finds a component that contains the files referenced in the INF file, a dependency on that component will be created rather than creating file resources. Econvert.exe does not. Another difference is that Econvert.exe determines the type of file being imported by the file extension. Component Designer lets you select the file types to browse for when importing a file. Typically Component Designer is the tool of choice for converting a file into an SLD file because it attempts to create a dependency on an existing component in order to include a file rather than creating a file resource. If a component exists that already includes the desired file or files, there is no need to clutter the database repository with duplicate files.

Section 9.2 Importing a PMQ file

Recall from the Target Analyzer chapter that a PMQ file is the type of output file generated by running either version of Target Analyzer on a system. These files can be imported into Target Designer as well as Component Designer. Importing the component into Component Designer creates a macro component, which is a collection of components grouped into one component by means of component dependencies. To import a PMQ file into Component Designer, select **Import** from the **File** menu, select **Target Analyzer files** from the **Files of type** pull-down menu, and then select a PMQ file. When the **Import file** dialog appears, specify a log file and click the **Start** button. It is similar to importing a PMQ file into Target Designer.

Section 9.2.1 Importing an INF file

An INF file contains setup information that is typically used with drivers, but can be used in installing applications and services. The setup information in an INF file includes the necessary information about the devices and files to be installed, such as driver images, registry information, version information, and so on. Importing an INF file involves the same steps as importing a PMQ file, except **Setup information files** is specified in the **Files of type** pull-down menu, and the **INF Processing Options** dialog appears before the **Import file** dialog. The **INF Processing Options** dialog enables you to select parsing options for the INF file.

The parsing options enable you to specify the sections of the INF file that you want scanned by the importer. For example, you may only want the importer to scan specific **AddReg** sections of the INF file.

Section 9.2.2 Importing a KDF file

A KDF file is a Windows NT Embedded 4.0 component definition file. It is created with the NT Embedded Component Designer. To make the migration from Windows NT to Windows XP, Windows XP Embedded Component Designer has the ability to convert an NT Embedded component into an XP Embedded component. An NT Embedded component contains files, registry data, and dependencies, just like an XP Embedded component. However, the dependencies are specific to NT Embedded, so when a KDF is imported into an SLD, an XP equivalent component will have to be found for an NT component dependency.

Importing a KDF file uses the same procedure as importing a PMQ file, except **Windows NT Embedded KDF files** would be selected in the **Files of type** pull-down menu. Because the KDF Importer contains pre-release code in this version of XP Embedded Studio, the KDF Importer is included as an add-in. To install the KDF Importer:

1. Copy all the files from the Windows XP Embedded CD folder **\VALUEADD\MSFT\PRERELEASE\KDFIMP** to the Windows Embedded utilities folder (<*Windows Embedded install directory*>\utilities).

2. To register the plug-in dll, open a command window, change directories to the Windows Embedded utilities folder, and then type **regsvr32 kdfimporter.dll**.

3. Import the KDF support definitions file, which is located in the Windows Embedded utilities folder, using Component Database Manager. Uncheck the **copy files** checkbox before importing.

Section 9.3 Component Authoring Tools and Techniques

Microsoft Windows Embedded Studio provides some capabilities to help create components using a file import method. If the file to be imported does not exist, there are some available third party applications that assist in gathering information for a component. These tools track changes that are made to the file system and registry as a driver or application is installed on the computer.

Section 9.3.1 System Snapshot Tools

The snapshot technique involves logging the contents of the file system and registry before the desired modifications are made to the system and again after the desired modifications have been made, and then comparing the two snapshots for changes to the system. A good snapshot should record every file and every registry key with its value. The dates of files should be examined as well in case a file has been replaced by a more recent file.

Sysdiff is one of the tools available that uses the snapshot technique. Sysdiff is a freeware command line tool available on the Microsoft OEM System Builder web site (http://oem.microsoft.com). The sysdiff.exe application uses a text file named sysdiff.inf to filter specified folders and registry keys, preventing them from being scanned. However, filtering out parts of the system from the scan may cause you to miss out on important system changes that occur as a result of making the desired system modification.

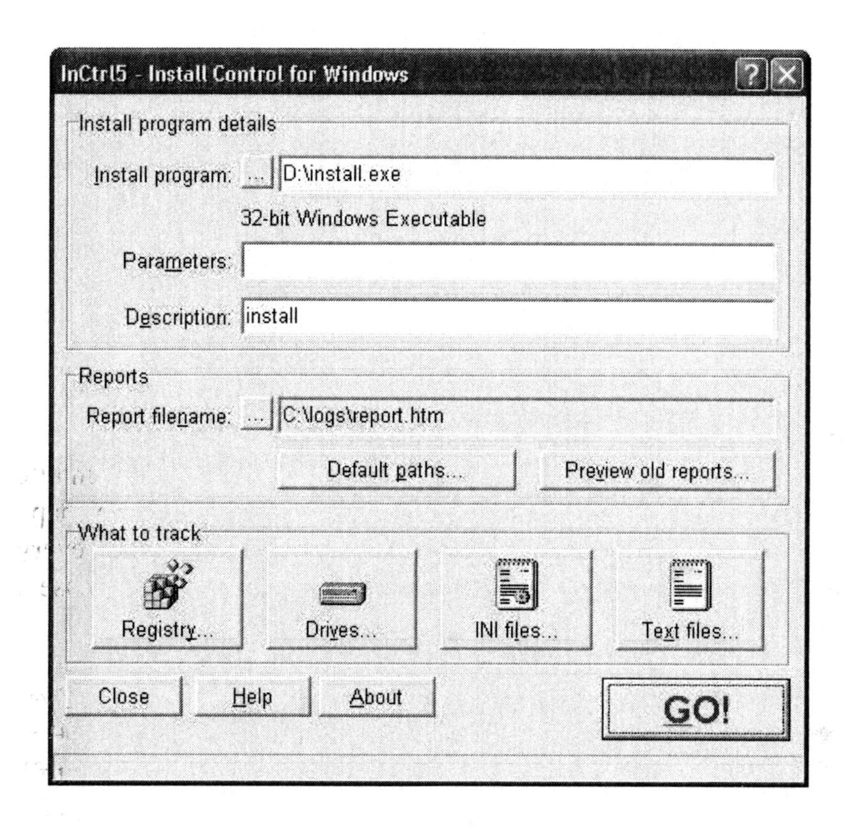

Figure 9.1 The Inctrl5 user interface.

Another tool that uses the snapshot technique is Inctrl5, available at http://www.pcmag.com. An installation executable is specified in the dialog of Inctrl5, along with some other settings pertaining to the system scan, and a report is produced that shows all the modifications made to the file system and registry.

Section 9.3.2 File System Monitoring: Filemon

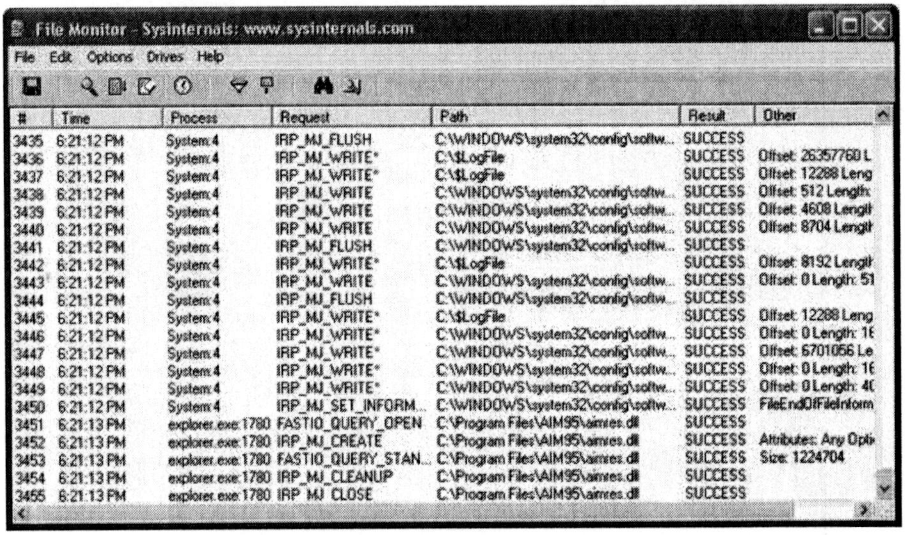

Figure 9.2 The Filemon user interface.

Filemon monitors and displays all activity of the file system in real time. Filemon not only shows the full path and filename of an active file, it also indicates the process that is using the file, the type of request on the file, the result, and other info. Each entry is numbered and time stamped. A filter can be applied so that selected folders or file can be included or excluded from the monitoring of the file system. It is recommended that you close any applications that you do not want to monitor file activity for. Filemon is a free tool that can be obtained at http://www.sysinternals.com.

Section 9.3.3 Registry Monitoring: Regmon

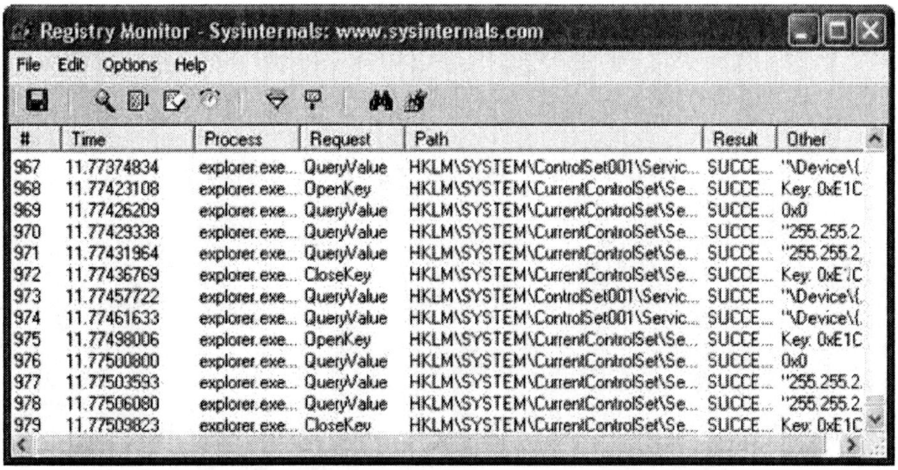

Registry Monitor - Sysinternals: www.sysinternals.com

File Edit Options Help

#	Time	Process	Request	Path	Result	Other
967	11.77374834	explorer.exe...	QueryValue	HKLM\SYSTEM\ControlSet001\Servic...	SUCCE...	"\Device\{
968	11.77423108	explorer.exe...	OpenKey	HKLM\SYSTEM\CurrentControlSet\Se...	SUCCE...	Key: 0xE1C
969	11.77426209	explorer.exe...	QueryValue	HKLM\SYSTEM\CurrentControlSet\Se...	SUCCE...	0x0
970	11.77429338	explorer.exe...	QueryValue	HKLM\SYSTEM\CurrentControlSet\Se...	SUCCE...	"255.255.2
971	11.77431964	explorer.exe...	QueryValue	HKLM\SYSTEM\CurrentControlSet\Se...	SUCCE...	"255.255.2
972	11.77436769	explorer.exe...	CloseKey	HKLM\SYSTEM\CurrentControlSet\Se...	SUCCE...	Key: 0xE1C
973	11.77457722	explorer.exe...	QueryValue	HKLM\SYSTEM\ControlSet001\Servic...	SUCCE...	"\Device\{
974	11.77461633	explorer.exe...	QueryValue	HKLM\SYSTEM\ControlSet001\Servic...	SUCCE...	"\Device\{
975	11.77498006	explorer.exe...	OpenKey	HKLM\SYSTEM\CurrentControlSet\Se...	SUCCE...	Key: 0xE1C
976	11.77500800	explorer.exe...	QueryValue	HKLM\SYSTEM\CurrentControlSet\Se...	SUCCE...	0x0
977	11.77503593	explorer.exe...	QueryValue	HKLM\SYSTEM\CurrentControlSet\Se...	SUCCE...	"255.255.2
978	11.77506080	explorer.exe...	QueryValue	HKLM\SYSTEM\CurrentControlSet\Se...	SUCCE...	"255.255.2
979	11.77509823	explorer.exe...	CloseKey	HKLM\SYSTEM\CurrentControlSet\Se...	SUCCE...	Key: 0xE1C

Figure 9.3 The Regmon user interface.

Regmon is a dynamic tracking tool like Filemon, but instead monitors all registry activity in real-time. It logs active registry keys and values, as well as the process that accesses the key or value, the request, the result, and other info. Each entry is numbered and can be time stamped or show the time that elapsed since you last cleared the output window or started Regmon. Additionally, Regmon can be configured to monitor boot time registry access. It configures itself as the very first driver to initialize in the system, which enables it to capture the registry startup activity of all other drivers and services. In this mode, registry activity is logged to a file named REGMON.LOG in the system root directory. Regmon is available for free at http://www.sysinternals.com.

Section 9.3.4 File Dependencies

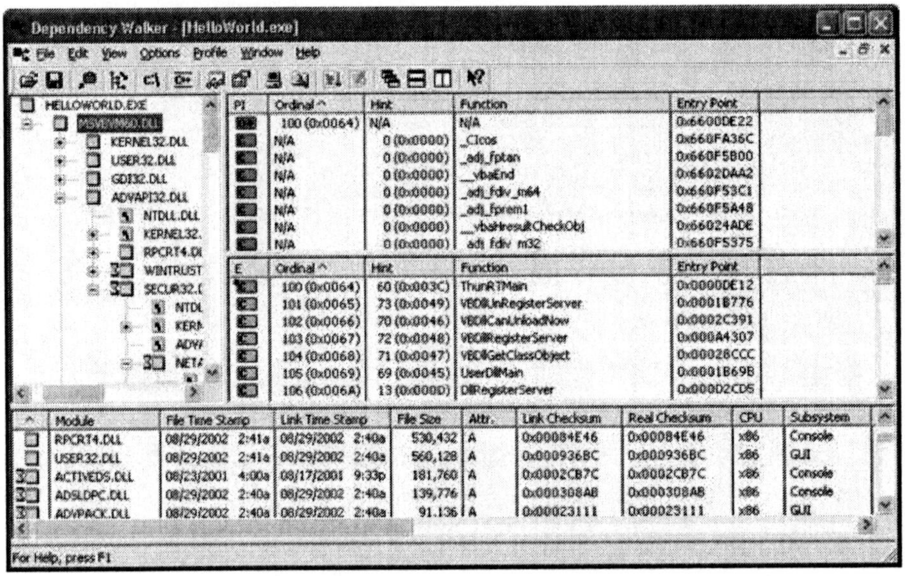

Figure 9.4 The Dependency Walker tool.

When creating a component it is critical to include all of the DLL files that are required for an application or driver. Dependency Walker is a useful tool that determines and lists all required DLLs required for an executable. Once the file's dependencies have been determined, the required files can either be included in the component or dependencies can be created on any existing components that already have the required files. Dependency Walker is included with the Microsoft Platform SDK which can be obtained from http://msdn.microsoft.com. Another binary files analyzer, Scanbin, can be downloaded for free at http://www.bel-lamyjc.net/en/scanbin.html. It basically performs the same tasks as Dependency Walker.

In the next exercise, Scanbin will be used to help create a custom shell component. The executable that will be used for the shell component is a simple Hello World application.

Section 9.4 EXERCISE 14

Setup for this exercise

1. Open **My Computer** from the **Start** menu and create the following two new folders:

   a. **C:\XPE dev\Hello SLD**

   b. **C:\XPE dev\Hello SLD\Rep**

2. From the **Windows XP Embedded** CD, copy the file **HelloWorld.exe** from the folder **\SAMPLES\TUTORIAL\HELLOREPOSITORY** to the folder **C:\XPE dev\Hello SLD\Rep**.

3. Download and install Scanbin from **http://www.bellamyjc.net/en/scan-bin.html**

Use Scanbin to determine the DLLs that HelloWorld.exe uses

1. After Scanbin has been downloaded and installed, launch Scanbin from **All Programs** in the **Start** menu.

2. Click the **OK** buttons on any dialogs that appear while launching Scanbin. The default values will suffice.

3. From the **Show** menu, **Used DLL list** and **Used DLL tree** will need to be selected. If there is not a check mark next to any of these items in the **Show** menu, click the item.

4. From the **File** menu, click **Binary file open**.

5. Browse to the folder **C:\XPE dev\Hello SLD\Rep**, select **HelloWorld.exe**, and then click the **OK** button.

Analysis of the Scanbin run

1. Click the **DLL used** tab in the output window.

Note: This tab lists all of the DLLs that are used by HelloWorld.exe. The list is divided into DLLs that are directly called by HelloWorld.exe and DLLs that are indirectly called by HelloWorld.exe.

2. Click the **DLL tree** tab in the output window.

Note: This tab displays all of the DLLs that are used by HelloWorld.exe in the form of a hierarchy tree that shows how each DLL is called by parent DLLs.

3. From either of these two views, note that HelloWorld.exe depends on one directly called DLL, msvbvm60.dll, and the following indirectly called DLLs:

    - advapi32.dll
    - gdi32.dll
    - kernel32.dll
    - msvcrt.dll
    - ntdll.dll
    - ole32.dll
    - oleaut32.dll
    - rpcrt4.dll
    - user32.dll

You do not need to know the purpose or function of any of these DLLs, only that they will be required by the system in order for HelloWorld.exe to function. In order to demonstrate how to find existing components that satisfy these DLL requirements, the remainder of this exercise assumes that you do not know anything about the DLLs.

Once it has been determined which DLLs are required for the application, the next step is to try to find components in the database that already include the required DLLs and then create an include dependency on such components in your component. If you are not able to find any such components, the DLL will have to be included as a file resource in your component. The best approach is to first try to find components which include the directly called DLLs. There's a high probability that any component which includes the directly called DLL will have a dependency on any components that include the indirectly called DLLs. Typically indirectly called DLLs, such as ntdll.dll and user32.dll, are used, directly or indirectly, by several other applications and libraries in the system. If you are not sure if the DLL in question is one of the common system DLLs, you can use the technique below to try to locate components which include the indirectly called DLLs.

Find the existing component that includes the required, directly called DLL msvbvm60.dll

1. Launch **Target Designer** and create a new configuration by clicking **New** from the **File** menu. This configuration will not be saved so it does not matter what the name is. It will only be used to locate and view components that are potentially required by the HelloWorld.exe application.

2. Open the Filter Manager to create a new filter by clicking the filter [funnel] icon in the component browser, and then click the **New** button.

3. Give the filter a name, such as **Filter for HelloWorld**.

4. Double click the filter rule **Component contains the following file: [filelist]** in the **Filter rules**.

5. Double click the filter rule in the **Filter description**, type in **msvbvm60.dll**, and then click the **OK** button.

6. Click the **OK** button.

7. Click the **Apply Filter** button.

8. The filter should have found the component **Visual Basic 6.0 Runtime Library** in the category **Software : System : System Services : Application Support**. Remember (or write down) the name and category of this component so that you can add it as an include dependency to the Hello World shell component that you will create later.

Note: If you are not able to see this component in the component browser, you might need to lower the component visibility threshold in the Target Designer options.

9. Double click the **Visual Basic 6.0 Runtime Library** component to add it to the configuration so you can examine its resources.

10. Expand the **Visual Basic 6.0 Runtime Library** component in the configuration editor and click on the **Files** resource. You can see that the component includes the required file **msvbvm60.dll**. Therefore, this component will become a dependency of the Hello World shell component that will be created later.

Now that a component was found that will satisfy the requirement of including the directly called DLL, msvbvm60.dll, the next step is to try to locate the components that include the indirectly called DLLs. The Visual Basic 6.0 Runtime Library component might have dependencies on other components which include the indirectly called DLLs. If so, then those components will not have to become dependencies of the Hello World shell component; they will be included through the Hello World shell component dependency on the Visual Basic 6.0 Runtime Library. Unfortunately there is no function or tool to determine the dependencies of a component. However, the method below can help determine a component's dependencies.

Find the dependencies of the Visual Basic 6.0 Runtime Library component and determine if they will satisfy the requirements for HelloWorld.exe

1. In Target Designer, make sure that the only component present in the configuration editor is the **Visual Basic 6.0 Runtime Library**.

2. Select **Options** from the **Tools** menu.

3. Click the **Dependency Check** tab, disable (uncheck) the **Auto-resolve dependencies** checkbox, and then click the **OK** button.

4. Select **Check Dependencies** from the **Configuration** menu.

5. Click the **Close** button when the dependency check is complete.

6. Resolve all of the dependency errors for the component **Visual Basic 6.0 Runtime Library**. Do not resolve the **Base Component** dependency error. With Auto-resolve disabled, each Visual Basic 6.0 Runtime Library dependency error requires you to add only one component. To resolve the dependency errors, double click on each one in the **Task** list (except for the Base Configuration dependency error) and click the **Add** button.

7. To determine if the newly added components would satisfy the DLL requirements of HelloWorld.exe, you will need to inspect the **Files** resource

of each component. The table below shows the HelloWorld.exe DLL requirements that are met by some of the newly added components:

DLL Requirement	Component
msvbvm60.dll	Visual Basic 6.0 Runtime Library
advapi32.dll	Win32 API – Advanced
gdi32.dll	Win32 API – GDI
kernel32.dll	Win32 API – Kernel
ntdll.dll	Primitive: Ntdll
ole32.dll	Primitive: Ole32
oleaut32.dll	Primitive: Oleaut32
user32.dll	Win32 API – User

Table 9.1 The HelloWorld.exe DLL requirements and the components that satisfy each requirement.

8. The dependencies of the Visual Basic 6.0 Runtime Library component satisfied all but two of the DLL requirements: msvcrt.dll and rpcrt4.dll. Another dependency check run with the newly added components might bring in components that include these two files. To run a dependency check, select **Check Dependencies** from the **Configuration** menu.

9. Click the **Close** button when the dependency check is complete.

10. Because there are many dependency errors, you can resolve the errors one at a time and check the **Files** resource as each dependency error component is added until you come across a component that includes one of the required DLLs. For this exercise, it was found that the **RPC Local Support** component, which is a dependency of the **Primitive: Ole32** component, satisfies the **rpcrt4.dll** requirement. The **Microsoft Visual C++ Runtime – Hotfix Q305601** component, which is a dependency of the **Primitive: Oleaut32** component, satisfies the **msvcrt.dll** requirement. (If you have not downloaded all of the QFEs from the Microsoft web site, which was an exercise

in the Component Database Manager chapter, your conclusions for satisfying the msvcrt.dll requirement may be different.)

11. Close Target Designer. When prompted to save the current configuration, click the **No** button.

12. Close Scanbin.

Based on the components and files that would be added by the dependencies and sub-dependencies of the Visual Basic 6.0 Runtime Library component, with the Auto-resolve dependencies feature enabled, it can be concluded that the HelloWorld.exe application requires only the Visual Basic 6.0 Runtime Library component. This information will be used to create the Hello World custom shell component in the next exercise.

Section 9.5 EXERCISE 15

Create a custom shell component for the HelloWorld.exe application using Component Designer

1. From the **Start** menu, select **All Programs**, select **Microsoft Embedded Studio**, and then click **Component Designer**.

2. Click **New** from the **File** menu.

3. From the **File** menu, click **Save As**.

4. Browse to the folder **C:\XPE dev\Hello SLD**, type in **Hello.sld** for the **File name**, and then click the **Save** button.

5. Expand the **Windows XP Embedded Client (x86)** node in the SLD browser.

6. Right-click on the **Repositories** folder and click **Add Repository**.

7. In the **Name** property, type **Hello World Shell repository**.

8. In the **Description** property, type:

```
This repository was created for HelloWorld.exe, which will be
used for the Hello World shell component.
```

9. Click the **Browse** button to the right of the **Source Path** property, browse to the folder **C:\XPE dev\Hello SLD\Rep**, and then click the **OK** button.

10. Expand the **Hello World Shell repository** in the SLD browser, right click on **Group Memberships**, and then click **Add Group Membership**.

11. When the **Add Repository Group Memberships** dialog appears, click the **Component Designer Exercises** package, and then click the **OK** button.

12. Right-click on the **Components** folder under the **Windows XP Embedded Client (x86)** node, and then click on **Add Component**.

13. In the **Name** property in the details pane, type **Hello World shell**.

14. In the **Description** property, type:

```
The Hello World shell component uses the HelloWorld.exe appli-
cation as the shell.
```

15. To specify a repository for the component, click the **Repositories** button to the right of the **Repository** property.

16. Click on the **Hello World Shell repository** and then click the **OK** button.

17. Click the **Browse** button to the right of the **Prototype** property.

18. Browse to the category **Software : System : User Interface : Shells**, click on the **Shell prototype component**, and then click the **OK** button.

19. Click on the **Advanced** button in the details pane and then click the **Add** button underneath the **Extended Properties**.

20. Type **cmiShellPath** in the **Name** field, select **String** from the **Format** pull-down menu, and then type **%SystemRoot%\System32\HelloWorld.exe** in the **Value** field.

21. Click the **OK** button on the **Extended Property** window, and then click the **OK** button on the **Advanced Properties** window.

22. Expand the **Hello World shell** component in the SLD browser.

23. Right click on **Files**, select **Add**, and then click on **File**.

24. Click the **Browse** button to the right of the Target Name property.

25. Browse to the folder **C:\XPE dev\Hello SLD\Rep**, click on the file **HelloWorld.exe**, and then click the **Open** button.

26. Click on the right arrow button to the right of the **Destination** property then click on %11%.

27. Click the **OK** button.

28. In the SLD browser, right-click on the **Component or Group Dependency** under the **Hello World shell** component, select **Add**, and then click on **Component Dependency**.

29. Browse to the category **Software : System : System Services : Application Support**, select the **Visual Basic 6.0 Runtime Library** component, and then click the **Apply** button.

30. Browse to the category **Software : System : User Interface : Shells : Windows Shell**, select the **Task Manager** component, and then click the **OK** button.

31. In the SLD browser, right-click on **Group Memberships** and then click on **Add Group Membership**.

32. Add the category group membership **Software : System : User Interface : Shells**. Expand the nodes using the + button, click on the **Shells** group, and then click the **Apply** button.

33. Under the **Dependency** folder, select the **Shell** dependency group and then click the **Apply** button.

34. Under the **Packages** folder, select the **Component Designer Exercises** package and then click the **OK** button.

35. Save the SLD file and close Component Designer.

Import the SLD file into the component database using Component Database Manager

1. From the **Start** menu, select **All Programs**, select **Microsoft Embedded Studio**, and then click **Component Database Manager**.

2. Click the **Import** button on the **Database** tab.

3. Click on the ellipsis [...] button to select the .sld file to import.

4. Browse to the folder **C:\XPE dev\Hello SLD**, select the file **Hello.sld**, and then click the **Open** button.

5. Click the **Import** button, and then click the **Close** button after the import process is complete.

6. Click the **Close** button to close the Component Database Manager.

Test the custom shell component in a run-time image

1. From the **Start** menu, select **All Programs**, select **Microsoft Embedded Studio**, and then click **Target Designer**.

2. From the **File** menu, click **Open**.

3. Browse to the folder **C:\XPE dev\TA_DATA**, select the configuration file **TAPPostImport.slx**, and then click the **Open** button.

*Note: If you did not save a post import copy of the TAP.exe-based configuration, TAPPostImport.slx, as was recommended in the Target Designer chapter, you need to import dev_tap.pmq into the configuration now. From the **File** menu, select **Import**, browse to the folder **C:\XPE dev\TA_DATA**, select **dev_tap.pmq**, and then click the **Open** button.*

4. From the **File** menu, select **Save As**.

5. In the **File name** text box, type **CustomShellDemo.slx** and then click the **Save** button.

6. Make sure that the **Auto-resolve dependencies** feature is enabled in the Target Designer tool options.

7. From the **Configuration** menu, click **Check Dependencies**.

8. Use the following table as a guide to resolve dependency errors:

Task	System Requirement	Resolution
Component: “Advance Configuration and Power Interface (ACPI) PC […]”	Boot loader.	Add “NT Loader” component.
Component: “Advance Configuration and Power Interface (ACPI) PC […]”	File system.	Add both “FAT” and “NTFS” components.
Component: “Compression and Expansion Tools[…]”	File system (duplicate).	Add both “FAT” and “NTFS” components.
Component: “Regional and Language Options […]”	Language support.	Add the “English Language Support” component.
Component: “Session Manager (Windows subsystem) […]”configuration.	Login process.	Add the “Windows Logon (Standard)” component.
Component: “User Interface Core […]”	Required utilities.	Add the “FAT Format” and “NTFS Format” components.
Component: “Windows Logon (Standard) […]”	Shell.	Add the “Hello World shell” component.

Table 9.2 Dependency Error Resolution

9. After completing the final dependency check with no errors, select **Build Target Image** from the **Configuration** menu.

10. Click the **Build** button. If prompted to perform a dependency check, click the **No** button. When prompted to delete all contents of the destination folder, click the **Yes** button.

11. Click the **Close** button after the build has successfully completed.

12. Save the configuration and close Target Designer.

13. Format the **D:** drive at **FAT**. WARNING! This will erase all data on D:!

14. Copy the contents of the destination folder, **C:\Windows Embedded Images** to the **D:** drive.

15. Make sure the **boot.ini** file in the root of the **C:** drive is set up for dual boot. It is assumed that this was done in the Target Designer chapter exercises.

16. Reboot the system.

17. When the system boots up, the HelloWorld.exe application should be the only thing that shows up. To shut down the system, press the **Ctrl**, **Alt**, and **Delete** keys on the keyboard at the same time to bring up the **Task Manager**, and then select the **Shutdown** option from the menu.

In this chapter you were introduced to tools and functions that help convert PMQ, INF, and KDF files into Windows XP Embedded component definition SLD files. You were introduced to some third party tools used to discover how an executable, application or driver installation or a change to a system setting affects the system registry and file system, as well as tools that determine the DLL dependencies of a binary file. Because there is no tool or function that can determine a database component's dependencies, you were shown a method that helped determine the dependencies of a component. Finally, the tools and methods that you were introduced to were used to create a custom shell component.

CHAPTER 10 Appendix A

Name [format]	Required/ Optional	Description
Component VSGIUD [GUID]	**N/A**	**Reserved for Microsoft**
MinRevision [integer]	**Required**	**Specifies the minimum required revision of the required component.**
TargetVIGUID [GUID]	**Required**	**Specifies the VIGUID of the replacement component**

Table 10.1 Component Branch Resource

Name [format]	Required/ Optional	Description
Component VSGIUD [GUID]	N/A	Reserved for Microsoft.
IdOriginal [Boolean]	Required	Reserved for Microsoft. Must be True.
IsCompatibleID [Boolean]	Required	Set to True if this is a compatible identifier as listed in the INF file for this device.
LowerFilter [Multi string]	Optional	Service names of lower filters that need to be installed for this device.
PnPID [String]	Required	Plug and Play identifier string as found in the INF file.
ServiceName [String]	Required	The device driver to be used for this device. Same as the string used under the HKEY_LOCAL_MACHINE\SYSTEM\ControlSet001\Services registry key.
UpperFilter [Multi string]	Optional	Service names of upper filters that need to be installed for this device.

Table 10.2 PnP Device ID Resource

Name [format]	Required/ Optional	Description
Component VSGIUD [GUID]	N/A	Reserved for Microsoft
Dependencies [Multi string]	Optional	Includes names of services or load ordering groups that the system must start before this service. Dependency on a group means that this service can run if at least one member of the group is running after an attempt to start all members of the group. A group string must be prefixed with a plus (+) sign, for example, +NetBIOSGroup, RpcSS.

Table 10.3 Service Data Resource

Name [format]	Required/ Optional	Description
ErrorControl [Integer]	Required	Specifies the severity of the error if this service fails to start during system startup, and determines the action taken if failure occurs. 0 = SERVICE_ ERROR_IGNORE – The startup program logs the error but continues the startup operation. 1 = SERVICE_ERROR_NORMAL – The startup program logs the error and displays a message box but continues the startup operation. 2 = SERVICE_ERROR_SEVERE – The startup program logs the error. If the last-known valid configuration is being started, the startup operation continues. Otherwise, the system is restarted with the last-known valid configuration. 3 = SERVICE_ERROR_CRITICAL – The startup program logs the error, if possible. If the last-known valid configuration is being started, the startup operation fails. Otherwise, the system is restarted with the last-known valid configuration.
LoadOrder-Group [String]	Optional	Name of the load ordering group of which this service is a member. If not specified then the service does not belong to a load ordering group.

Table 10.3 (Continued)Service Data Resource

Name [format]	Required/ Optional	Description
Password [String]	Optional	A string that contains the password to the account name specified by the StartName property. Leave blank if the account has no password or if the service runs in the LocalService, NetworkService, or LocalSystem account. Ignored for driver services.
ServiceBinary [String]	Required	Path to the executable file for the service. Note the following guidelines: Use parameterized path names (DIRIDS), such as using %11% to represent the effective path C:\Windows\System32. You do not need to use quotation marks to enclose spaces in the file path.You can include additional arguments to your executable file following the executable name. Do not use hard-coded values for any files you may reference in your argument files. You do not have to supply the full path for the files in your argument as long as they are found in the search path on the run-time image. If you have an INF file that defines your service, this string can be the identical string you have in your INF file.
ServiceDescription [String]	Optional	Description of the service. If you are using text in your INF file, use the same text here.

Table 10.3 (Continued)Service Data Resource

Name [format]	Required/ Optional	Description
ServiceDisplayName [String]	Optional	Displayed to the user as the name of the service. If you are using text in your INF file, use the same text here.
ServiceName [String]	Required	String that uniquely identifies your service. This is the service key name that is recorded in the registry for this service, and the other parameters are written under this key for the service. The Windows XP service control manager database preserves the case of the characters, but service name comparisons are always case insensitive. Forward-slash (/) and backslash (\) are not valid service name characters.

Table 10.3 (Continued)Service Data Resource

Name [format]	Required/ Optional	Description
ServiceType [Integer]	Required	Type of service. This is a value derived by combining (using the OR operator) the following masks: 16 = SERVICE_WIN32_ OWN_PROCESS (= 0x00000010) – Specifies a service that runs in its own process. 32 = SERVICE_WIN32_ SHARE_PROCESS (= 0x00000020) – Specifies a service that shares a process with other services. 1 = SERVICE_KERNEL_DRIVER (=0x00000001) – Specifies a driver service. 2 = SERVICE_FILE_ SYSTEM_DRIVER (=0x00000002) – Specifies a file system driver service. If you specify SERVICE_WIN32_ OWN_PROCESS or SERVICE_ WIN32_SHARE_PROCESS, you can also specify the type. 256 = SERVICE_INTERACTIVE_ PROCESS (=0x00000100) – Enables a service to interact with the desktop.

Table 10.3 (Continued)Service Data Resource

Name [format]	Required/ Optional	Description
StartName [String]	Optional	Name of the account under which the service is to be run. If the service type is SERVICE_WIN32_OWN_PROCESS, use an account name in the form *DomainName\UserName*. The service process will be logged on as this user. If the account belongs to the built-in domain, you can specify *.\UserName*. If this parameter is not specified, the service is started under the LocalSystem account. If ServiceType specifies SERVICE_INTERACTIVE_PROCESS, the service must run in the LocalSystem account. If this property is set to NT AUTHORITY\LocalService, the LocalService account is used. If you specify NT AUTHORITY\NetworkService, the NetworkService account is used.

Table 10.3 (Continued)Service Data Resource

Name [format]	Required/ Optional	Description
StartType [Integer]	Required	Specifies when the service is to be started. 0 = (SERVICE_BOOT_START) – Indicates a driver started by the OS loader. This value should be used only for drivers or devices required for loading the OS. 1 = (SERVICE_SYSTEM_START) – Indicates a driver started during OS initialization. 2 = (SERVICE_AUTO_START) – Indicates a driver or service started on demand, either by the Plug and Play manager when the corresponding device is numerated or by the Service Control Manager in response to an explicit user demand. 3 = (SERVICE_DEMAND_START) – A service started by the service control manager when a process calls the Win32 StartService function. 4 = (SERVICE_DISABLED) – Indicates a driver or service that cannot be started.

Table 10.3 (Continued)Service Data Resource

Name [format]	Required/ Optional	Description
Arguments [String]	Optional	Specifies the command line arguments, if any, to pass to the application specified in the *FilePath* property. Arguments containing paths should be specified using parameterized path names (DIRIDS), such as using %11% to represent the effective path C:\Windows\System32.
ComponentVS-GUID [GUID]	N/A	Reserved for Microsoft.
FilePath [String]	Required	Specifies the path and file name of the executable file. This value must be a fully qualified path, using parameterized path names such as %11%\MyRunOnce-App.exe.
Flags [DWORD]	Required	Indicates which one of the three registry keys that the program specified in the *FilePath* property will be listed: 0 = Run 1 = RunOnce (default) 2 = RunOnceEx
ValueName [String]	Required	Specifies the name of the program to run. In the registry, this is the name of the REG_SZ value used to specify the program name.

Table 10.4 RunOnce Request Resource

Name [format]	Required/ Optional	Description
Arguments [String]	Optional	Command line arguments that are to be passed to the program specified in the *FilePath* property. Arguments using paths should use parameterized path names (DIRIDS), such as using %11% to represent the effective path C:\Windows\System32\.
ComponentVSGUID [GUID]	N/A	Reserved for Microsoft.
ErrorControl [Integer]	Required	Controls how the FBA handles errors when executing the program specified in the *FilePath* property: 0 = Continue on error (default) 1 = Halt on error If the CreateProcess return value or the process exit code is greater than 0x80000000, then the FBA considers this an error and behaves according to the value of this property.
FilePath [String]	Required	Specifies the path and name of the program to be executed. This value must be a fully qualified path, such as %11%\cmd.exe. Use parameterized path names.

Table 10.5 FBA Generic Command Resource

Name [format]	Required/ Optional	Description
Flags [Integer]	Required	0 = Create the process and wait for the number of seconds specified in the *Timeout* property for it to exit before continuing. (default) 1 = Create the process and continue.
Reboot [Boolean]	Required	True = The FBA will complete its operation, reboot, and then continue. False = The FBA continues to process without rebooting. (default)
Start [Integer]	Required	Reserved for Microsoft. Must be 1.
Timeout [Integer]	Required	Indicates the number of seconds that a program is allowed to execute before the FBA terminates it. 0 = Infinite (default) Ignored if the *Flags* property is set to 1.
Type [Integer]	N/A	Reserved for Microsoft. Must be 1.
Phase [Integer]	Required	Indicates when the command will be run during the FBA. In most cases, this value should be set at 8500. If the processing needs to occur after cloning, the value should be set at 12000.

Table 10.5 (Continued)FBA Generic Command Resource

Name [format]	Required/ Optional	Description
Argument [String]	Optional	Specifies the value for the pszCmdLine parameter passed to the *DLLInstall* entry point. Arguments using paths should use parameterized path names (DIRIDS), such as using %11% to represent the effective path C:\Windows\System32\. (default is an empty string)
ComponentVS-GUID [GUID]	N/A	Reserved for Microsoft.
DLLInstall [Boolean]	Required	True = The *DLLInstall* entry point is called. Both *DLLInstall* and *DLLRegister* can be set to True. False = (default)
DLLRegister [Boolean]	Required	True = Either the DllRegisterServer or the DllUnregisterServer entry point is called based on the value of the *Flags* property. Both *DLLInstall* and *DLLRegister* can be set to True. (default)
ErrorControl [Integer]	Required	Controls how the FBA handles an error when processing an operation: 0 = Continue on error (default) 1 = Halt on error If the return value of LoadLibrary, GetProcAddress, or the DLL entry point is greater than 0x80000000, then the FBA considers this an error and behaves according to the value of this property.

Table 10.6 FBA DLL/COM Registration Resource

Name [format]	Required/ Optional	Description
FilePath [String]	Required	Specifies the path and name of the DLL to be loaded. This value must be a fully qualified path, such as %11%\MyDll.dll. Use parameterized path names (DIRIDS).
Flags [Integer]	Required	This property is a bit-mask that is interpreted as follows: Bit 0 – specifies which entry point is called first: DllRegesterServer/DllUnregisterServer or DllInstall. If set, then DllInstall is called first. Bit 1 – Specifies the type of operation to be performed. If *DllRegister* is set to True and this bit is 0 then DllRegisterServer is called, otherwise DllUnregisterServer is called. If *DllInstall* is set to True and this bit is 0 then DllInstall(True,<*Arguments*>) is called, otherwise DllInstall(True,<*Arguments*>) is called. The default value of this property is 0.
Reboot [Boolean]	Required	True = The FBA will complete its operation, reboot, and then continue. False = The FBA continues to process without rebooting. (default)
Start [Integer]	Required	Reserved for Microsoft. Must be 1.

Table 10.6 (Continued)FBA DLL/COM Registration Resource

Name [format]	Required/ Optional	Description
Timeout [Integer]	Required	Indicates the number of seconds that registration operation is allowed to take before the FBA terminates it. 0 = Infinite (default)
Type [Integer]	N/A	Reserved for Microsoft. Must be 2.

Table 10.6 (Continued)FBA DLL/COM Registration Resource

The following table will help clarify how the various combinations of Flags, DllInstall, and DllRegister FBA DLL/COM Registration resource properties are interpreted:

DllRegister	DllInstall	Flags	Effect
False	False	0	N/A
True	False	0	DllRegisterServer
False	True	0	DllInstall(TRUE)
True	True	0	DllRegisterServer followed by DllInstall(TRUE)
False	False	1	N/A
True	False	1	DllRegisterServer
False	True	1	DllInstall(TRUE)
True	True	1	DllInstall(TRUE) followed by Dll-RegisterServer
False	False	2	N/A
True	False	2	DllUnregisterServer
False	True	2	DllInstall(FALSE)
True	True	2	DllUnregisterServer followed by DllInstall(FALSE)
False	False	3	N/A
True	False	3	DllUnregisterServer
False	True	3	DllInstall(FALSE)
True	True	3	DllInstall(FALSE) followed by DllUnregisterServer

Table 10.7 FBA DLL/COM Registration resource Scenarios

Name [format]	Required/ Optional	Description
Component VSGUID [GUID]	N/A	Reserved for Microsoft.
DLLEntry-Point [String]	Required	Specifies the name of the function in the OC Manager helper DLL.
ErrorControl [Integer]	Required	Controls how the FBA handles an error when processing an operation: 0 = Continue on error (default) 1 = Halt on error If the return value of the DLL entry point is greater than 0x80000000, then the FBA considers this an error and behaves according to the value of this property.
FilePath [String]	Required	Specifies the path and name of the OC Manager helper DLL responsible for installing the optional component. This value must be a fully qualified path, such as %11%\cmd.exe. Use parameterized path names.
GroupName [String]	Required	Specifies the name of the parent component group. Optional components can belong to more than one parent group.
INFName [String]	Required	Specifies the INF file that contains the install section associated with this optional subcomponent.

Table 10.8 FBA OC Mgr Request Resource

Name [format]	Required/ Optional	Description
OCName [String]	Required	Specifies the name of the subcomponent. The subcomponent belongs to a parent component group.
Phase [Integer]	Required	Indicates when the command will be run during the FBA.
Reboot [Boolean]	Required	True = The FBA will complete its operation, reboot, and then continue. False = The FBA continues to process without rebooting. (default)
Start [Integer]	Required	Reserved for Microsoft. Must be 1.
Timeout [Integer]	Required	Indicates the number of seconds that operation is allowed to take before the FBA terminates it. 0 = Infinite (default)
Type [Integer]	N/A	Reserved for Microsoft. Must be 3.

Table 10.8 (Continued)FBA OC Mgr Request Resource

Name [format]	Required\ Optional	Description
Arguments [String]	Optional	Command line arguments passed to the application invoked by the shortcut. Arguments using paths should use parameterized path names (DIRIDS), such as using %11% to represent the effective path C:\Windows\System32\. (default is an empty string).

Table 10.9 Shortcut Resource

Name [format]	**Required\ Optional**	**Description**
Component VSGUID [GUID]	N/A	Reserved for Microsoft.
DstName [String]	Required	Name of the LNK file that is generated for the shortcut. The LNK file is the actual shortcut file.
DstPath [String]	Required	Path which specifies where the shortcut will appear in the file system. Parameterized paths should be used, such as using %16409% to place a shortcut on the desktop for all users.
HotKey [String]	Optional	Assigns a hot key combination to a shortcut, which will enable the shortcut to invoke its application by pressing a combination of the keys assigned to this property. The syntax is [*KeyModifier*]*Keyname*. *KeyModifier* can be ALT, CTRL, or SHIFT. The *KeyName* can be a letter key (a through z), a digit (0 through 9), or a function key (F1 through F12), and is not case sensitive.
IconLocation [String]	Optional	Assigns an icon to the shortcut. This is specified as the name of an executable file on the target system followed by a comma and an icon resource identifier. For example, Notepad.exe,0. A default icon is assigned by Windows XP if one is not specified here. It is typically the icon resource with identifier 0 in the target executable file of the shortcut.

Table 10.9 (Continued)Shortcut Resource

Name [format]	Required\ Optional	Description
Overwrite [Boolean]	Required	TRUE = Target Designer will overwrite an existing shortcut file that has the same name in the same location. FALSE = (default)
TargetPath [String]	Required	Path and file name of the application invoked by the shortcut. Use parameterized path names, such as %16409%\Notepad.exe to create a shortcut for Notepad.
Window-Style [Integer]	Required	Determines the window style for the application invoked by the shortcut. It can be one of the following: 1 = Activates and displays a window. If the window is minimized or maximized, the system restores it to its original size and position. 3 = Activates the window and displays it as a maximized window. 7 = Minimizes the window and activates the next top-level window.
WorkDir [String]	Optional	Specifies the initial working directory for the application invoked by the shortcut.

Table 10.9 (Continued)Shortcut Resource

Index

Numerics

802.11 5

A

adding components 78
Applicable build types 123
applications 1
ARC path 100
authorized distributors 21
auto-resolve 95

B

blue screen of death 101
Boot.ini 90
Bootable CD-ROM 180
Bootprep, see also bootprep.exe 6
bootprep.exe 17, 25
build options 20
Build process
  overview 12

C

Command shell 146
Component Authoring Tools 198
Component Branch Resource 217
Component Browser
  defined 76
  List View 77
  Tree View 77
component build order dependency 125
Component Conversion 195
Component Database Manager 6, 14
  defined 25
  launching 45
component definition files 47
component dependencies, adding 137
Component Designer 6, 13
  defined 24
Component Designer interface 106
Component DHTML 115
component object, creating 135
Component Properties 114
  Prototype 114
  Repository 114
Component resources 83
Component Tab 52
component, defined 52
configuration 13
Configuration Editor 79
connectivity 5
custom objects, creating 107
custom shell component, creating 209
custom shells, testing 213

D

Database Engine Setup 23, 25, 29
Database Setup 23, 26, 30
Database Tab 46
Dependencies 129

Dependency
- Build Order 125
- component build order 125
- Component or Group 124
- group build order 125

Dependency check 87
- defined 14
- performing 94

dependency errors 95
Dependency Walker tool 202
Deployment 15
Destination property 120
Details Pane 81, 106
development system requirments 8
Device Driver Rollback 3
DHTML, component 115
DIRID 120
distributors, authorized 21
DLLs
- determining 203
- directly called 204
- finding components 205
- indirectly called 204

Document Type Definition, see DTD
drivers 4
DTD 71
dual booting 89

E

Econvert.exe 195
Effective path 120
El Torito Bootable CD-ROM 180
El Torito run-time image, building 185
End-Of-Life 126
Enhanced Write Filter 5, 165
- Components and Files 167
- settings 168
- testing 179

etprep utility 192
EWF
- Demo 171
- Disk Number 170
- Disk Type 170
- Enabled 169
- Lazy Write 169
- Optimization Option 170
- Overlay Type 170
- Partition Number 170
- Volume 167

EWF Manager Console application 167
EWF NTLDR 167
EWF, see also Enhanced Write Filter
Ewf.inf 168
Ewfdll.dll 168
ewfmgr 179
exclusive mode 46
Explorer shell 146
Extended Property, adding 108
Extensible Markup Language, see XML

F

FBA DLL/COM Registration 128
FBA DLL/COM Registration Resource 229
FBA DLL/COM Registration Resource Scenarios 232
FBA Generic Command 128
FBA Generic Command Resource 227
FBA OC Mgr Request 128
FBA OC Mgr Request Resource 233
FBA, see First Boot Agent
FBALOG.txt 167
features, XP Embedded 3
File Dependencies 202
file references, adding 135
File System Monitoring 200

Filemon 10, 200
Files, adding 118
Filter Manager 53
Filter Tool 53
filter, creating 54, 55
firewall 3
First Boot Agent
  booting image 183
  defined 18
  system booting 191
  system initialization 90
Flash Media 180
footprint 4

G
Globally Unique Identifier, see GUID
graphics subsystem 147
group build order dependency 125
Group memberships 117
  adding 139
GUID 107, 111

H
HARDWAREIDS 72
Hd2iso tool 183
Hd2iso.exe 181
Headless Operation 5, 147
  BIOS 147
  System Message Interception 148
headless system, defined 147
Headless VGA Driver 147

I
IIS FTP Server 149
image size, reducing 173
Inctrl5 199
INF files
  converting 195
  importing 196
Installation Scenarios 26
Internet Protocol Security, see IPSec
IPSec 3
IrDA 5
Iso Image, advanced options 189

K
KDF files
  defined 197
  importing 197
KDF Importer 197
Kerberos security 3

L
licensing 20
LogSeverity 159

M
macro component 116
  defined 77
MessageBox 155
Microsoft Message Queuing 5
Mode 85
MSDN 58
multi-user scenario 39

N
new application component, creating 131
non-volatile media 5
NT Embedded 4.0 6

O
Opaque 116
overlay
  Disk 166
  RAM 166
Overlay Types 166

P

package object, creating 133
Package Tab 51
Packages 113
  defined 113
performance 3
Platform Tab 50
PMQ 14
PMQ files 66
  converting 195
  importing 196
  reading 71
PnP Device ID 127
PnP Device ID Resource 218
product id key 21

R

read import mode 46
reduce image size 173
Registry Branch 121
Registry Data 121
registry data, adding 121, 136
registry hive files 110
Registry Monitoring 201
Registry path 123
Regmon 10, 201
remote connection, testing 153
Remote Desktop Connection 154
Remote Desktop Protocol 5
Remote Management 5, 148
  connecting 149
  IIS FTP Server 149
  including components 150
  Telnet Server 148
Remote Recover 18
Repositories 51
  adding 111
  build and debug 112
  creation and use 111
  defined 110
Repository 112
repository object, creating 134
Repository Properties and Resources 112
Repository Set
  defined 112
Reseal phase 19
Root pull-down menu 123
RunOnce Request 127
RunOnce Request Resource 226
run-time image
  deploying 97
  transferring 17
Run-time Image Licensing 92

S

Scanbin 10
  using 203
SDI Manager 25
security 3
Service Data Resource 219
Shell Customization 145
shortcut resources, adding 138
Shortcut Resource 234
Simple Network Management Protocol 150
SLD Browser 106
SLD files
  defined 105
  importing 140, 212
SLD files, see also component definition files
SLX, see System Level Configuration
SNMP 150
SQL Server 2000
  authentication mode 40
  installing 40
  login ID 42
  user accounts 41
  user ID 42
Sysdiff 198
system cloning 19

System Cloning Tool 19
System Level Configuration 13
System Level Definition (SLD) file, creating 132
System Level Definition file, see SLD
System Message Interception 148, 155
System Requirements 7
System Snapshot Tools 198

T

TA.EXE 25, 66
TA.EXE and TAP.EXE 66–73
  Command Prompt Parameters 68
  compared 66
TAP.EXE 25, 66
TAP.exe output file, importing 90
TAPI 3.1 5
Target Analyzer 6
  overview 65
Target Designer 6, 75
  Component Browser 75
  Configuration Editor 75
  defined 24
  Details pane 75
  Output pane 75
Target Designer Options 84
  Advanced 88
  Build 86
  Dependency Check 87
  Mode 85
Target Device Settings 100
target media
  preparing 16
  structure 15
Target System requirements 9
Task Manager shell 146
Terminal Server Remote Desktop 149
Terminal Services Core 147
test build 92
third party software 10
Tools Setup 23, 35
Troubleshooting Tips 100
True Flash File System 15

U

Universal Plug and Play 5
User Interface Core component 103

V

VGA Boot Driver 147
Visibility 116

W

WBEM 149
Web-Based Enterprise Management 149
Win32 API 4
Windows Driver Protection 3
Windows Embedded Studio 6, 12
Windows File Protection 3
Windows Management Instrumentation 149
Windows NT Embedded 4.0 197
Windows Product Activation (WPA) 21
Windows Update 3
Windows XP Embedded Desktop 102
Windows XP Embedded Updates 58
wireless LAN 5
WMI 149

X

x86 50
XML 66